THE EXPERIENCE DESIGNER

Every one who has a desire to improve their own process of learning should spend some of their precious time with this book. This is simply the best book that I have read on the process of learning. The Experience Designer *begins by making us conscious of our own narratives, critical thinking, and creativity, and asks us to question the assumptions we have about learning and education. We then walk through network learning environments where we use our inventiveness, cleverness and imagination to interact with a wide variety people, places and things. The design and implementation of network learning environments are a distributed responsibility serving to promote diversity in learning.*

Finally, we explore the interactive process of designing hardware and software tools to support human ingenuity. His vision is unique, risky, and compelling. This is essential reading for anyone interested in taking charge of the future of learning.

Jerome Durlak, Communication Arts Professor, York University and the Canadian Film Centre

Brian Alger has raised the bar significantly. By challenging all of us as learners and designers of learning to assess our current systems for education and training, he encourages us to make fundamental changes. Thoughtfully implemented, these shifts in thinking and practice will unleash the largely untapped power of e-technologies to help design authentic, interactive learning experiences for students, teachers, trainers, trainees and learners everywhere.

Bob Williams, Education Leader; Director of Education

With The Experience Designer, *the author goes beyond the conventional notion of e-learning to provide us with a comprehensive context for lifelong and personal evolution. I highly recommend this book to everyone with an interest in learning. Brian empowers us to take control of the learning process through his holistic, systematic and inventive approach. This excellent volume should be on every educator's desk!*

Robin G King, President IMAGINA Corporation; Sheridan College Digital Animation Program

D1366503

THE EXPERIENCE DESIGNER

LEARNING, NETWORKS AND THE CYBERSPHERE

BRIAN ALGER

2002 First Edition

Published by Fenestra Books™
610 East Delano Street, Suite 104
Tucson, Arizona 85705, U.S.A.
www.fenestrabooks.com

International Standard Book Number: 1-58736-092-6
Library of Congress Control Number: 2002101049

Cover design by Atilla L. Vékony

Printed in the United States of America

For the spirit and people of Enduring Freedom everywhere

THE EXPERIENCE DESIGNER:
LEARNING, NETWORKS AND THE CYBERSPHERE

TABLE OF CONTENTS

Table of Contents

PREFACE:
E-LEARNING HAS YET TO BE
INVENTED

The Experience Designer is a vision for the future of e-Learning. It embraces and clarifies new potential for learning, networks and the cybersphere. *The Experience Designer* is a work of creative nonfiction designed to inspire thought leaders and creative people throughout the corporate, government, education and cultural sectors. The crisis of e-Learning is looming on the horizon; the current practices and tools for e-Learning are neither sustainable nor durable. In our present day, the e-Learning industry faces fundamental challenges for survival.

> **E-Learning is the most powerful force influencing the evolution of the Internet. The potential of e-Learning cannot, however, be realized without a vibrant conception of learning. Businesses, governments, education systems and cultural enterprises focused on the mass production and distribution of information bits and bytes through e-Learning are destined for extinction.**

The subtitle—*Learning, Networks and the Cybersphere*—is the symbol for a creative system of thought resulting in new strategic directions for e-Learning. The real source of design for *e-Learning* is a vibrant conception of the word *learning*. The gap between *learning* and *e-Learning* is wide. The reason for this is clear: the industrial-age practices still dominating our education and training systems have seduced the innovative possibilities of e-Learning. The gap between *networks* and *educational design* is wide. The potential of the Internet as a learning environment has been seduced by the mechanized and automated traditions of instructional design. The *Cybersphere* refers to the Internet surrounding e-Learning and the interplay between authentic experience and digital experience. *Learning, Networks and the Cybersphere* represents the structure and flow of thought in *The Experience Designer*.

> *Learning, education and training are different ideas. E-Learning, e-Education and e-Training are different design processes. The creative opportunity for e-Learning has been dramatically limited by digital retrievals of old practices.*

1

The people involved in e-Learning include government policy makers, corporate leaders, university professors, new media designers, information technology experts, educational leaders, employees, students and parents. Corporations are embracing *e-learning, corporate intranets, electronic performance support, knowledge management* and *data mining* as a means to improve organizational performance. Governments are developing policies to support ideas such as *lifelong learning, employability skill, competencies for all, globalization,* and *smart communities* in order to help prepare and support people throughout their participation in society. Educational institutions are adopting new delivery systems to support the ideas of *distance education, on-line courses, virtual schools* and *mobile learning* in order to extend their educational reach and capacity. Cultural institutions are developing strategies for *digital heritage, intercultural communications, cyber-art* and *cultural innovation* in order to promote cultural identity and diversity. The electronic embrace of e-learning reaches into any location with Internet access.

Before we attach the letter "e" to learning we need to first ensure that our conception of "learning" is in fact useful in order to make certain that we do not develop sophisticated electronic products based on ideas that are less than useful.

In a society where the time to reflect and reconsider our basic assumptions and habits is nearly nonexistent, we are in fact accelerating ourselves in directions that have not been clarified or understood effectively. *E-Learning* is one such idea—it is a land of confusion. At the same time, it is an idea that I believe has profound potential for the future evolution of the Internet. In fact, I would dare to say that e-Learning *is* the future of the Internet. This book, then, departs from traditional trade publications designed to provide quick solutions, summaries of existing practices and consulting opportunism. *The Experience Designer* is intended to inspire thought and ideas in the critical and creative thought leaders of our time in order provide vibrant lifelong and lifewide learning experiences. I am appealing to thought leaders, or those people who are engaged in critical reflection and creative practices regardless of their particular area of expertise. These are the people who clearly understand that the essence of designing our future lies in deep, creative and reflective thinking. The human phenomenon of learning and how it can be supported via e-Learning is *not* a simple idea.

The typical corporate definition and value proposition for e-Learning is an illusion. The reason for this is that their work is premised

2

on the production and sale of technology rather than the improvement of learning.

The source of design for e-Learning in this environment quite naturally originates in the need to sustain revenues. In other words, the corporate realm simply cannot articulate a systemic vision of e-Learning that reaches beyond the practical realities of their own business plan. The marketing language of e-Learning, in keeping with the long tradition of commercial propaganda, often heavily borrows from notable educational researchers and innovators as a means to create an impression. In spite of the highly fictional and hallucinatory language of many e-Learning value propositions, it does not take long to realize that e-Learning in our present day originates in a revenue stream. Needless to say, this is the reality of being in business, but it is also to say that the ability for an e-Learning business to reconsider e-Learning in visionary terms is limited to sales tactics and marketing documents.

The new paradigm for e-Learning described in The Experience Designer **presents a critical challenge to current practices as well as an opportunity to invent the future.**

Just as *learning* is a more comprehensive idea than *education* or *training*, *e-Learning* is a more comprehensive idea than *e-Education* or *e-Training*. For corporate, government, educational and cultural e-Learning programs, policies and products to be strategic and durable they must originate in a *source of design* that is centered on a vibrant concept of *learning*, and not in our traditional ideas of education and training.

The inspiration for a truly visionary conception of e-Learning is absent, in spite of the propaganda that surrounds it in the commercial world. Unless we collectively evolve our thinking, a powerful and fundamental force of change on the Internet may fade into oblivion.

In *The Experience Designer* is a campaign for e-Learning intelligence. The current patterns of traditional education and training practices must be recalibrated for the power of e-Learning to be released on the Internet. Ultimately, my work is an invitation to a system of thoughts and ideas that clarify the future of e-Learning.

Brian Alger, 2001

INTRODUCTION:
E-LEARNING INTELLIGENCE

The Experience Designer is an invitation to the reader to engage in an innovative system of thinking that explores, invents, imagines, probes, provokes, and builds ideas about e-Learning. The thoughts in this book are a collage of critical, creative, hopeful, and skeptical probes that are coordinated into a new system of thought and a new vision for e-Learning.

Learning is the most critical human resource and source of stability for the unavoidably lifelong and lifewide confluence of modern life. It is obvious to say that learning occurs over the entire course of our lives. We learn whether we want to or not; it is as much about the things we remember as it is the things we forget, the things we are aware of and the things we are unaware of, the things we do and the things we do not do, the things we make and the things we destroy, and the things we consider to be good and evil. Learning is simultaneously a public concourse and a private discourse.

Networks are a very powerful force in modern life. Network phenomena have a pervasive influence on our corporations, governments, educational institutions and cultural organizations. The real source of design for network design is learning, not technology. The interactive domain leads us to consider a unified approach to learning through networks that facilitate a broad range of communication and exploration across a global repertoire of people, places and things.

The Cybersphere is a term used to capture the cross-media electronic surroundings of the Internet. The purpose of an e-Learning system is to capture, integrate and facilitate the optimum range of possibilities and opportunities for *learning* and *networks*, or *network learning*. In other words, any meaningful approach to the design of e-Learning systems originates in a rich and vibrant conception of network learning.

Part One: Learning

The idea of *learning* throughout the Experience Designer refers to the lifelong and lifewide experiences of people. The universal motivation for learning is the quest for individual and collective identity. Education and training programs, in contrast, are commonly motivated by information acquisition and skill development. The human phenomenon of *learning* is far more magnificent and powerful than either education or training.

Chapter 1: Narrative and Modern Life

The idea of *narrative* is at the nucleus of what *learning* means. Learning is fundamentally a quest for building connections and relationships that promote stability in our lives. Stability is learned through the development and preservation of our private and public *identity*. Our interface with experience is our identity, or how we construct our stories about our *connections with and relationships to* the world we live in.

> ?   *"How did I (can I, will I) learn the things that I have valued the most in my life?"*

> ?   *"How did we (are we, will we) learn the things that we will value most in our lives?"*

Information is a completely inadequate source of design for learning. Regardless, it is also the predominant source of design in many education and training programs. Current practices in education and training that emanate from curriculum as information design, instruction as information delivery, and standardized assessment as a right of passage to accreditation are ineffective. The solution is to position the power of narrative as the source of design. In doing so, we are invited into a process of paradigm pioneering.

Chapter 2: Critical Vitality

Critical vitality is a cluster of thinking styles and events that are designed to clarify our current situations and circumstances so that a new foundation for growth, improvement and innovation can be established. The purpose of critical vitality is to clarify the underlying assumptions, tacit conditions, habits and traditions that define the structure and therefore the experiences in our lives.

> *?*　*Who will value my ideas (methods, rules, policies, organizations, systems, etc.) and how can I communicate this value to them in a rational manner?*

> *?*　*Whose ideas (methods, rules, policies, organizations, systems, etc.) are these and how can I determine what value they really have to me?*

Critical vitality is the synthesis of critical thinking and critical action. It represents a fundamental source of energy for the construction and preservation of the narratives that guide our private and public lives.

Chapter 3: Creative Vitality

Creative vitality is a cluster of thinking styles and events that result in the design, construction and expression of new contexts, situations and circumstances. The purpose of creative vitality is to make and build structures and organizations that promote growth and innovation in practical terms. Critical vitality is the synthesis of creative thinking and creative action.

> *?*　*What can I design, build and take action on in order to promote new strategic directions for personal growth?*

> *?*　*What can we design, build and take action on in order to promote new strategic directions for public growth?*

The complete integration of both critical and creative vitality is essential in building a narrative. Without critical vitality, our narratives will wander into an abstract and disconnected representation of things (i.e. doing in the absence of thinking). Without creative vitality, our narratives will deteriorate into mere armchair abstraction (i.e. thinking in the absence of doing).

Part Two: Networks

A network is a system of interaction that facilitates the creation of connections and relationships across a diversity of people, places and things over time. It is *not* an idea that merely refers to the physical hardware and software used to support the Internet. A *network* is a means to structure and coordinate powerful sets of environmental conditions for learning.

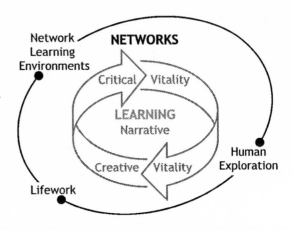

Chapter 4: Network Learning Environments

A *network learning environment* focuses learning on the creation and strategic use of connections and relationships. It is a coordinated set of situations and circumstances for learning that empowers the learner to create and evolve a range of experiences across people, places and things. In other words, the learner is intimately involved in shaping the learning environment to support their own motivations for learning. The means to coordinate a network learning environment is called *interaction design*.

> *?* **What are the optimum conditions to support learning through networks?**

A network learning environment requires us to reconsider the nature of power, control, authority, responsibility and entitlement in learning. The result is not an extension of traditional classroom practices that organize learning through information typologies, but a completely different paradigm for instruction.

Chapter 5: The Network Explorers

All learners are explorers; we do not learn unless we explore. To observe a person learning is to view the ways in which they are exploring their present circumstances. The most fundamental and important aim of any instructional design methodology is to promote the improvement of abilities such as investigating, discovering and inventing. Improving the learner's capacity for *exploration* is the single most important reference point for instructional design. The primary objective of the instructional designer is to establish lifelong and lifewide structures for the development of human ingenuity.

> *?* **What are the most essential and fundamental abilities for learners to develop in order to fully leverage network learning environments?**

Our world is rich with narratives of people making discoveries and embarking on quests and journeys. These are not merely stories to be read, but more importantly they comprise a fundamental repertoire of real-life methods, models, processes, and tools for exploration in authentic situations and circumstances. If we were to build a generic set of "skills" that were aimed at being universal, nothing less than human ingenuity would provide a strong enough foundation.

Chapter 6: Lifework

Lifework is the guiding philosophical force for our use of networks. It is the practical, concrete and observable representation of our learning as seen throughout our daily lives. As an economic strategy, lifework is the single most important means to design and construct a systemic support system for employability skills and career directions.

> *?* **What is the underlying ground for living a creative and fulfilling life?**

The idea of employability is reduced to the mere acquisition of isolated and transient skills sets, or competencies. The idea of a career is often a reactive response to existing opportunities in the workforce. Lifework is a fundamental point of reference for making decisions about employment and career management.

Part Three: The Cybersphere

The Cybersphere is the electronic gathering place for network learning. More specifically, a series of new ideas can now be developed as a direct result of the foundation established in Parts One and Two. The basis of a new paradigm for e-Learning emerges here.

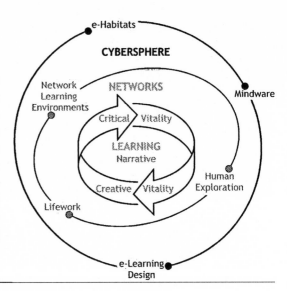

Chapter 7: e-Learning Habitats

The most important design consideration for e-Learning is to think of it as a unique kind of electronic habitat within the more comprehensive idea of a *network learning environment.* An e-Learning environment is primarily designed to facilitate *human ingenuity.*

> *?* **How can the idea of e-Learning be restructured in order to promote more innovative and creative approaches for learning?**

The use of old education and training paradigms within new technological environments is, unfortunately, a well established norm. E-Learning has been needlessly reduced to ways of delivering information and traditional course structures on-line. In intellectual and economic terms, this approach is not sustainable.

Chapter 8: Mindware

E-Learning is dependent upon the critical and creative vitality we bring to our use of Internet technology. The ways of using networked software is first and foremost a creative act than it is a technical act with respect to learning.

> *?* **What is the most effective use of software to support learning?**

The technological realizations of such software entities as learning management systems, reusable information objects, and courseware authoring systems are all built on a transient set of assumptions. These modern day software development initiatives are examples of how new technologies can further entrench old paradigms of thought.

Chapter 9: e-Learning Design

The future of e-Learning technology requires a network learning environment that integrates the corporate, government, education and cultural sectors. The rationale for this is based on the following: a) no one sector has the necessary intelligence to evolve e-Learning to new levels of value and performance; b) learning is a source of design that transcends any one sector; and c) network technologies are most effectively developed by powerful, adaptive and flexible networks of relationships.

> *?* **What are the design requirements that lead directly to new and innovative practices in e-Learning?**

In the end, the e-Learning design results in a unified and distributed array of network tools that are combined and repurposed in response to the needs of the learner.

A Vision for e-Learning

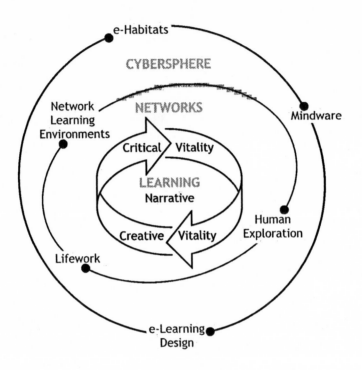

PART ONE: LEARNING

Thought Process

The purpose of *Part One: Learning* is to establish a durable, sustainable and consistent frame of reference for the experience we call *learning*.

At the center of this frame of reference is *Narrative and Modern Life,* or ways in which we can establish stability in the confluence of modern life. *Critical Vitality* and *Creative Vitality* are the two most fundamental sources of passion and motivation for learning.

Taken together, these elements form the nucleus of the phenomenon of learning. It is a model of learning that provides the foundation for *Part 2: Networks* and *Part 3: The Cybersphere.* It is of primary importance to develop a vibrant and durable conception of learning *prior* to any consideration of e-Learning.

Probes

! The mastery of information in the absence of narrative is a recipe for the mastery of ignorance.

! Learning has little to do with education and training.

! Information is a problem to be eliminated.

! The experiences of real people in real circumstances are the single most important source of "content" for learning.

! Curriculum is a means to reduce people to standardized information.

Overview

Chapter 1: Narrative and Modern Life

Our lives are completely immersed in the creation of narratives, or ways of explaining ourselves to ourselves. The stories we tell form our public and private identity. They are the essence of who we are, whether it takes the form of a lifestyle, a corporate brand, a novel, a television program, a military campaign, a government policy, or an artistic enterprise. The idea of narrative as a means to create and communicate identity is the nucleus of learning.

Stability
We are all on a lifelong quest for stability. Somewhat enigmatically, stability is attained by remaining flexible and adaptable throughout the unavoidable confluence of modern life. Remaining proactive in the face of changes in our circumstances is the most powerful way to celebrate our private and public identities.

Interactivity
Interactivity is the real alphabet of our narratives. Our narratives are created through the people we communicate with, the places we find ourselves in, and the things that we value. The range of people, places and things in our lives converge to create a diversity of circumstances and situations.

Mobility
The mobility of mind, body and spirit is essential to learning. When we are mobile we are strategically searching for new kinds of experiences in our lives. Mobility is the medium for learning.

Chapter 2: Critical Vitality

Critical vitality represents the collection of thoughts and actions that allow us to clarify our experiences so that new conditions for growth and innovation can be established.

Competencies
A competency is a transient and disposable skill that people master in order to perform a task or activity.

Capacities
A capacity refers to the optimum conditions, requirements, and opportunities for the development of human potential.

Capabilities

A capability is a shared human interest and need that leads to clear and concrete improvement in local, regional, national and global spheres.

Chapter 3: Creative Vitality

Creative vitality represents the multitude of ways in which we design, build, construct and invent new contexts, situations and circumstances that lead to growth and innovation.

Effectiveness

For creativity to be effective it must be connected to practical and meaningful results. The raw materials of creativity are the circumstances of modern life.

Improvisation

Improvisation, or creating new opportunities and possibilities out of the situations we find ourselves in, is the leading edge of creative vitality and a superior strategy for bridging the gap between thinking and action.

Achievement

The end result of creative vitality is the evolution of our identities, a greater resolve in the face of life's challenges, and a greater sense of unity within ourselves as well as across the spectrum of cultural diversity.

1. NARRATIVE AND MODERN LIFE

The idea of *narrative* is at the nucleus of what *learning* means. Learning is fundamentally a quest for building connections and relationships that promote stability in our lives. Stability is learned through the development and preservation of our private and public *identity.* Our interface with experience is our identity, or how we construct our stories about our *connections with and relationships* to the world we live in.

"How did I (can I, will I) learn the things that I have valued the most in my life?"

"How did we (are we, will we) learn the things that we will value most in our lives?"

Information is a completely inadequate source of design for learning. Regardless, it is also the predominant source of design in many education and training programs. Current practices in education and training that emanate from curriculum as information design, instruction as information delivery, and standardized assessment as a right of passage to accreditation are ineffective. The solution is to position the power of narrative as the source of design. In doing so, we are invited into a process of paradigm pioneering.

Chapter Design

Stability
Learning is a means to build stability—or the durability and adaptability of our private and public identity—in our lives. It is the essence of who we are, whether it takes the form of a personal lifestyle, a corporate brand, a government initiative, or a cultural enterprise.

Interactivity

Interactivity embodies all narratives. It is constructed from the range of people we interact with, the places we find ourselves in, and the things that we value. The boundaries of interactivity are determined by the sum total of the intended and unintended events that take place in our lives.

Mobility

Mobility is a fundamental requirement for the flow of learning and a core concept for the use of technology. By expanding the breadth and depth of our narratives through mobility, an increased demand is placed on providing a wide range of variety in the place and space of learning.

The title for this book—*The Experience Designer*—comes from the world of the interactive artist and is the symbol for the experience we refer to as *learning*. The benefit of thinking about learning in this way is to provide a fresh foundation for rethinking a number of assumptions and biases we consciously and subconsciously maintain, as well as to develop strategic directions and tactical approaches that can liberate our thinking, institutions, organizational designs and activities. In this sense, *The Experience Designer* is in itself an experience designed *to provide a lot of material for the audience [you] to participate in.*

> *For a number of years I've wanted to become an experience designer rather than just a musician and this new technology is one of the things that is going to allow us to take a first step in that direction. Interactivity is exciting because it helps us not just to be artists but to provide a lot of material for the audience to participate in—so that eventually they become the artists themselves and can use what we create, in a sense as collage material, as stuff to explore and learn about from the inside. (Gabriel, Peter 1993)*

Learning is a private and public quest for stability in the face of the confluence of modern life. It is a phenomenon that is different from both education and training. For the most part, education has tended to be a reactive system designed to try and keep pace with social and economic change. Similarly, training is a highly reactive system designed to provide mastery in skills that are perceived as an immediate need or requirement for success. While these reactive systems have a kind of utility, they are generally disconnected, fragmented and lack coherence for people over time. This reactivity, however, is a very natural and normal outcome of systems that are designed to respond to external changes that are largely outside their own realm of influence and control. At its most fundamental level, it is a problem that originates from intellectual assumptions that are biased by information, mechanization and automation. *The Experience Designer* embraces and clarifies a new set of assumptions about learning.

The idea of designing experiences invites all participants into a world of authentic *narrative* creation and preservation, the human ecology of *interactivity*, and the private and public *mobility* of our mind, body and spirit. Traditionally, we tend to think of learning (and therefore education and training) in terms of lesser aims such as *knowledge, skills* and *attitudes*. The aims of learning here are elevated to *narrative, interactivity* and *mobility* and provide the nucleus of experience design. If learning is to be a "solution" to anything, it must emanate from ideas about stability, durability and sustainability in the face of change and innovation. The three aims of learning provide this sense of stability and are therefore a means to feel less reactive, anxious and adrift in the confluence of modern life. They are also a means to rethink, recalibrate and redesign systems for education and training.

There is a great deal of writing dedicated to the criticism of current practices in education. There have been and are in existence a great many innovative projects with new approaches to schooling and training. In spite of this, systemic change in our approaches to education and training has been difficult to sustain over time. What is it that holds great ideas from durable implementation? In our present time, many of our assumptions about learning remain mired in an information mindset. The main difference between the industrial society and the information society is that we have replaced the assembly line with the information line. The ever-widening gap between how we are educated and trained and what is being genuinely experienced in modern life results in a never-ending story of falling behind and catching up. We need to ask the question, "What are we really falling behind in, and why should we believe that it is important to catch up to it?" The lack of a practical connection between the alphabetic voyeurism of education and training and the authentic experience of learning is a defining characteristic of the *primacy of information*.

> They're (myths) stories about the wisdom of life, they really are. What we're learning in schools is not the wisdom of life. We're learning technologies, we're getting information. There's a curious reluctance on the part of faculties to indicate the life values of

> *their subjects. . . . Specialization tends to limit the field of prob-*
> *lems that the specialist is concerned with. . . . The generalist gets*
> *into range of other problems that are more genuinely human than*
> *specifically cultural. (Campbell, Joseph 1988)*

Information is a narcissistic predator of attention in the digital age. By its very nature, *information is unstable.* The *problems that are more genuinely human* referred to by Joseph Campbell are those that are anchored in our everyday experiences. What Campbell reveals with his unrelenting clarity is the gap that exists between the experience of education and the experience of everything else in our lives. In other words, the kinds of challenges and prob-lems we are presented with in education originate in information theory rather than having a direct correlation with the confluence of modern life. To a degree, information overload and anxiety can be linked to the general state of our private and public emotional health (n.b. the issue of mental health is of course far more complex than this). For example, the percentage of our population suffering from debilitating emotional states such as violence and depression have to some degree been ill-equipped by their education and training to deal with the realities of modern life. Corporate and public edu-cation curricula that ignore or confine the confluence of modern life to information prisons are not helpful. People are often incorrectly labeled by society if they tend to embrace problems that are *more genuinely human than cultural.* Information is safer than modern life, but this sense of safety is mis-leading. The increased violence in our schools and places of work not only intensifies the need for better safety and surveillance systems, but a critical need for more strategic and aggressive approaches to helping people deal with reality.

A recent article in *Newsweek* indicated a serious problem with teacher recruitment in the United States. It indicated that the USA will require 2 million new teachers during the first decade of 2000, but may not be able to supply them. To compound the problem, 20% of teachers leave the profes-sion after the first three years, and 33% leave after five years. The reasons commonly cited by teachers who have left are money, irresponsible students, apathetic parents and long hours. The article quite intelligently focused on trying to capture a talented but dissatisfied teacher's reasons for the problem:

> *I am a picture of confusion, dumbfounded inadequacy, panic, fail-*
> *ure and guilt. Regardless of how many hours I give, I always feel*
> *like I could have/should have given more. So why do I do this?*
> *(Kantrowitz, Barbara 2001)*

The emotional context described above is one of mild depression. How is it that a healthy, motivated and talented teacher can be transformed into a picture of mental unrest in the period of a few years? One reason for this is that the primacy of information as it is imposed through curriculum creates a huge gap between people and what it is they are required to learn. Standardized testing is nothing more than an admission that the curriculum lacks relevance. The teacher above is quite literally trapped in an information concentration camp that is designed to isolate and control them. It is perfectly natural for this person to become depressed, and in fact we might say that *not* becoming depressed under these conditions is a clear sign of mental illness.

Learning, education and training are not the same things. Seeking stability in the confluence of modern life demands narrative. Education demands the acquisition of pre-determined and isolated categories of knowledge, skill and attitudes. Training demands the mastery of generic techniques and methods. It is entirely possible to successfully avoid being educated or trained in life, but it is not possible to avoid learning. In other words, it is not possible to avoid one's personal narrative in life, the public narrative that we find ourselves in, interacting with a diversity of people, places and things, and developing mobility of mind, body and spirit. It is, however, possible not to do these things well, and therefore feel unsettled and insecure in our lives. *The Experience Designer* embraces learning in three concrete and practical ways: a) the creation and preservation of our private and public narratives; b) improving the human ecology of interaction; and c) attaining greater levels of mobility in mind, body and spirit.

Stability

Learning is intimately connected with narrative—the key to the making of our private and public identity.

How did you learn the things you value most? The answer to this question at a general level is, "The things that I value the most are embedded in personal stories that illuminate the essence of who I am." The only authentic and genuine learning environment is the entire breadth and depth of our lives. The private and public narratives we make and destroy are the primary source of motivation and relevance in learning:

We do not discover ourselves in myth; we make ourselves through myth. Truth is constructed in the midst of our loving and hating; our tasting, smelling, and feeling; our daily appointments and weekend lovemaking; in the conversations we have with those to whom we are closest; and with the stranger we meet on the bus. Stories from antiquity provide some raw materials for mythmaking, but not necessarily more than the television sitcoms we watch in prime time. Our sources are wildly varied, and our possibilities, vast. (McAdams, Dan 1993)

The phrase "we *make ourselves* through myth" has some important implications. A myth is something we use to build our identity; it is a medium for inventing and reinventing ourselves to ourselves. In this sense, a modern-day myth is a story each of us builds in order to create our *identity.* It points to the essence and the embodying character of who we are at that moment in time. While there are many kinds of stories that do not attempt such depth of thought and meaning, a myth is the highest achievement of storytelling. I have used the word *narrative* instead of *myth* and *story* throughout *The Experience Designer.* In other words, *a narrative is the active living process of creating individual and cultural identity through myths and stories.*

The narrative focuses us on the present moment and circumstances of modern life, explores the past in order to seek clarification of modern life, and constructs strategic directions to design the future. A narrative is not merely a fanciful story or literary technique.

The sentence, "Our sources are wildly varied, and our possibilities, vast," centers us in the fact that the confluence of modern life is the underlying ground for narrative. For example, a corporation is inescapably tied to narrative as is a writer. Science and technology themselves are fundamentally narratives once we are able to see beyond their plethora of methods and techniques. A narrative is inexorably bound to the present moment, draws from the experiences of the past, and invents the future. In the end, all media, technology, scientific methods, business plans, economic issues, government policies and the like constitute a repertoire of raw materials from which to create narratives. As stand-alone entities, they have little power to communicate. The narrative places us unavoidably in the path of understanding the entirety of the present moment as a means to explore the past and the future.

Learning does not occur in the absence of narrative. A narrative is an act of critical thinking, creative thinking, communication design, perceptual acuity, authenticity, and applied knowledge. It follows then that the essential character of learning is one of building identity by creating meaning from the present, drawing from the past, and continually inventing and reinventing the future. The narrative is the most natural and genuine intellectual network of human interactivity. It cannot be institutionalized, bureaucratized, mechanized, automated, contained in or confined by information typologies, subject disciplines and courses of study. In other words, the narrative is the most fundamental liberating structure for learning available to us.

All acts of learning originate in the private realm of the individual. This is in contrast to the acts of education and training which originate outside the realm of the learner. The word *student* is a symbol and archetype for kinds of learning that do not originate in the individual but are imposed by a *teacher*. A *learner* can play the role of student or teacher when relevant to do so, but both a *student* and a *teacher* are something less than a *learner*. With respect to learning we refer to the participants as *learners*; with respect to education we refer to the participants as *students*; and with respect to training we refer to the participants as *trainees*. These distinctions in language are important in helping to distinguish the acts of learning, education and training from each other.

Learning is an experience aimed at the creation of authentic narratives that clarify the present, draw from the past and invent the future. Education is an experience aimed at the understanding of information typologies, or subject disciplines, that are designed to provide the basis for entry into society and citizenship. Training is an experience aimed at the mastery of methods and techniques in order to successfully complete specific tasks and activities as efficiently as possible.

Learning is not some mystical activity. In fact, children are far more adept at creating authentic narratives since their frame of reference for the world has not been limited by types and categories of information even though their breadth of experience and cognitive maturity is limited by their age.

The pursuit of information and knowledge in the absence of an authentic narrative is a powerful strategy for the comprehensive mastery of ignorance.

There is, however, a problem and therefore a risk in the way in which the word *narrative* is sometimes understood as being soft, fictional, fanciful, not serious, and unscientific. In other words, it is an idea that is often categorized under the general heading of "Humanities" and is not commonly referred to in "Science and Technology." Further compounding the problem, the word *myth* is often thought of as a fanciful story about ancient gods. If this were the way in which both narrative and myth are understood, then they do not form a useful foundation for thinking about learning. However, the use of the word *narrative* throughout this book refers to an ability to connect the sum total of our experiences (intellectual, informational, emotional, technological, social, scientific, cultural, spiritual and economic) into a stable flow of meaning that connects our lives within ourselves to others. To put it in the simplest and clearest terms, the ways in which we use our technologies, apply scientific invention and method, and use mathematical formulae are as much an aspect of narrative as our literature, music, visual art and entertainment. A narrative is never merely fictional; it is always a work of critical and creative nonfiction. The *hardness* of information is given meaning through the *softness* of improvising experience. Narratives are the means by which we privately and publicly create our lives.

> **At its summit, a narrative clarifies what we know, how we came to know it, and what we do about it.**

The power of narrative as a concrete and practical strategy for growth and improvement can be referenced against four interrelated dimensions of modern life: a) corporate; b) government; c) education and d) cultural. These four dimensions are not the sum total of our experience, but are flexible reference points selected for the discussions throughout *The Experience Designer*. For corporations, a narrative is a means to unify vision with operations, strategy with profitability, and planning with results. For governments, a narrative is a means to unify policy with practice, budgeting with improvement, and organizational design with practical activity. For education, a narrative is a means to unify theory with practice, information and knowledge with meaningful application, and abstraction with experience. For cultural enterprise, a narrative is a means to unify policy with practice, institutions with growth and improvement, universalism with realism, and globalism with diversity. The creative dimension of narrative building is the recognition of patterns of experience and their meaning. The analytical dimension of narrative building is understanding the past precedents and events that clarify the present. The strategic dimension of narrative is the plan we design for improving the future.

Dan McAdams' *The Stories We Live By* is an essential frame of reference for understanding the fundamental importance of narrative creation as a primordial and instinctive human capacity for constructing identity. The construction of identity is simultaneously a private (personal, interior, individual) activity as well as a public (community, organizational, cultural) activity. The private and the public ebb and flow with each other. An education that does not help people to create and construct their identity will force them to wallow in the sea of information without any larger purpose or connection. The psychological impact of the primacy of information as seen through the endless timetabling of subject disciplines does not seek to unify our experiences in life. People and their experiences are not mere information typologies, as the primacy of education as information would seduce us into believing. Neither are so-called multidisciplinary or interdisciplinary studies; these are merely variations on the theme of information. However, if these kinds of information were given a new sense of connectedness and guidance through a deep and sensitive understanding of narrative, we would arrive at a basis for rethinking our educational system.

A critical direction for education is to replace the assumption of information as curriculum with the assumption of narrative as curriculum.

How do we learn the thing we value most? A common reaction is to reflect upon important experiences in our lives. The first experiences that come to mind are likely births, deaths, health, love, leisure, sports, money, and business. The way you characterize these events, consciously and unconsciously, dramatically informs your own view of the world and your place in it. Some of my experiences have been happy while others have been traumatic—the same is probably true for you. These experiences are the basis for the beliefs, attitudes and ideas that forced us to a personal crossroad—when we crossed the intersection between what was and what we must now face, for better and for worse. Unless we choose to grow and evolve as an individual from these experiences, we become less of ourselves. In a creative life we feel experiences and take action as much as we think about them. If we are uncreative in our lives, we feel an underlying sense of loss and wandering. The resulting narrative is discontinuous and fragmented. *The lifelong and lifewide process of creating and evolving a narrative is the essence of learning; learning is fundamentally an act of authentic narrative building.*

Our genius lies in our capacity to make meaning through the creation of narratives that give point to our labors, exalt our history, elucidate the present, and give direction to our future. (Postman, Neil 1995)

Where do information and knowledge fit into a narrative? If learning is about creating and expressing meaning in our lives then information must be sensibly and sensitively connected to that experience. The problem with the primacy of information is not in the fact that learning involves remembering information. There is nothing inherently wrong with rote learning (learning through repetitive practice in order to develop a habit) and memorization of facts in the right situation. The problem lies in the fact that information has absolutely no value in our lives unless we relate and connect it to a narrative. Rote learning and memorization do not achieve this sense of connectedness as an end unto itself. If we only rote learn information, then we may remember it effectively but not understand or use it well. The desire to make our experiences transparent in order to *understand and give meaning* is a different sensibility than the desire to *remember* information.

Authentic narratives integrate all kinds of information, but are not confined by status quo categories, topics and subjects. We don't learn stories by sitting and listening to them being read to us; we learn them by recreating the story in relation to our own lives. Plot, characterization, setting, mood and the other analytical tools have little relevance and importance in the pursuit of meaning. *A story is not a mere body of information to be dissected, remembered and regurgitated; it is a model for thinking about living.* The most profound and useful narratives originate in authentic experience.

"I like the spiritual feeling of being on a mountain," he says. "The space. The sounds. The vast openness of it. The most annoying question I get is, 'Why climb when I can't see the view from the top?' You don't climb for the view. No one suffers the way you do on a mountain for a beautiful view. The real beauty of life happens on the side of the mountain, not the top." [Weihenmayer, 2001 #64]

Erik Weihenmayer is blind. This glimpse into his story, wonderfully captured in *Sports Illustrated* magazine, focuses on the superficial enigma of the "blind mountain climber." There is no enigma, except for the fact that some people in our society might think there is one. The experience of climbing Everest (www.everest2001.com) is not something that requires sight, technically, physically or emotionally. Erik further comments, "I want to summit, and I like the pioneering aspect of being first. For me, though, the process is more fun, the moments of bliss that connect you with who you are. The summit is just a symbol that on that day you brought an uncontrollable situation under control." What is even more apparent is that Erik is consciously following and building his own private narrative and extending it to the public realm. *Erik Weihenmayer's narrative is an archetype of learning in the confluence of modern life.*

Weihenmayer is living the hero's journey as described by Joseph Campbell:

It's important to live life with the experience, and therefore the knowledge, of its mystery and your own mystery. This gives life new radiance, a new harmony, a new splendor. Thinking in mythological terms helps to put you in accord with the inevitable of this vale of tears. You learn to recognize the positive values in what appear to be the negative moments and aspects of your life. The big question is whether you are going to be able to say a hearty yes to your adventure. (Campbell, Joseph 1988)

At thirteen years of age, Erik became blind. In Campbell's terms, this was Erik's *mystery* of everyday life and *the inevitable vale of tears.* "Once he went blind and accepted it, he had a whole new platform from which he could grow," his father says. "Erik says that blindness is an incredible adventure, and that's the mind-set you have to have." [Weihenmayer, 2001 #89] Erik is a teacher in the deepest sense of the word, since he crafts his life to serve as a model for others. He has put himself *in accord with the inevitable of this vale of tears* and he has said *a hearty yes* to his adventure. In addition to his personal adventure, he had another purpose in mind. Being the first blind person to attempt Mount Everest attracts public attention and interest. Erik's public narrative demonstrates the keen ability of a blind person in parallel with the development of an awareness that approximately 70% of the blind are unemployed. Due to the social ignorance surrounding blindness, Erik had been turned down in three attempts at obtaining a dishwashing job. On May 25, 2001 he reached the highest point on earth, the summit of Mount Everest.

Of course, none of the above is to say that subject content, expertise, knowledge, information and skill development no longer have a role (n.b. I will refer to this collection as *subject disciplines*). But the role of the subject disciplines must be subservient to the power of narrative. If we look at the story of Erik Weihenmayer through the filter of subject disciplines, it is a simple task to connect them to history, science, art, and so on. The moment we do this, however, we are engaged in an analytical and reductionist approach, in spite of the fact that we might call it *multidisciplinary* or *interdisciplinary*. The immediate impact of this is to isolate parts in the flow of the story and remove them from their context. This can be a great advantage if we deepen our understanding about a particular perspective and then revisit the flow of the story to see if we develop new meaning and purpose from it. In other words, the information must be recontextualized in the authentic and genuine flow of the narrative to have value.

The Internet is a collection of electronic raw material for the construction of individual and collective identity. The *effective use* of ICT (Information and Communications Technology) is guided and given direction by this fundamental purpose. A core capability for using the Internet is to develop capabilities, capacities, and competencies for crafting narratives. In this sense, the Internet is really a kind of grammar for the creation of electronically networked identities. If the Internet were thought of as a kind of story, then we see that it consists of a setting (*cyberspace*), plot (called *digital interactivity and communications*), characters (called *users* and *avatars*), episodes (called *web events* and *web-casting*), props (called *web pages, web sites* and *web tools*), goals (a range of objectives such as *searching, collaborating,* and *conferencing*), and consequences (called the *effects of the Internet on people and society*). If the WWW is empty of people exploring, building, capturing, archiving, connecting, creating, sharing, linking, disseminating, representing, designing, displaying, expressing, and communicating individual and collective narratives, myths and stories to guide people's lives in an open and transparent manner, then it remains nothing more than the electronic mastery of ignorance.

The same can be said of other media. The telephone, the television, the car, the train, and all other technologies that facilitate physical and intellectual mobility also constitute raw materials for building narratives, but they are not a story unto themselves. If we bias the Internet with information categories, then we accelerate and distribute increasing levels of fragmentation and isolation that inevitably result from the absence of narrative. The presence of information in itself is not a problem, but the lack of connection to private and public identity is a serious problem. *Efficient use of the Internet is aligned with the language of access and information. Effective use of the Internet is aligned with narrative-centered approaches to learning.*

It is useful to consider the ideas of lifelong education and lifelong training. *Lifelong education* in the sense I have described above would mean that a person is involved in a series of teacher-student relationships over the course of his or her life that are designed to improve and upgrade the knowledge, skills and attitudes required for successful participation in society. The imposed knowledge, skills and attitudes often originate in a reaction to economic change. *Lifelong training* would mean that a person masters transient skills that are designed to inculcate specific methods and techniques in the least amount of time. Since there is a degree of utility in both forms, our corporate, government, education and cultural institutions would quite naturally embrace them. Training keeps people up to date in methods and techniques. Education upgrades people's knowledge, skills and attitudes toward growth initiatives through courses and programs of study. *Learning, however, is the fundamental source of unity and coherence for education and training.*

The creation and preservation of authentic narratives is the source of design for learning.

The development of organizational design and implementation models for education as narrative would require dramatically new structures, financial strategies, social policies, evaluation practices, professional development, curriculum designs, and instructional strategies. It is not in any way an issue of throwing away information, but it is about taking information typologies and placing them into an entirely new intellectual and organizational context. Is this not the essence of creativity—the courage and ability to place ourselves into new contexts so that we may learn more deeply? Intensifying and accelerating the existing information paradigms of education and training will only serve to magnify violence, mental illness, networked bureaucracies, corporate ignorance, cultural misunderstandings, illiteracy, social inequuities, impotent hero figures, and a general feeling of disconnection from a larger sense of purpose in life. This is not to say that the narrative is some kind of panacea that will magically solve all of our problems—it will not. It is, however, a fundamental and essential strategic direction for growth and improvement.

Interactivity

The difference between *an experience designer* and *just a musician* as described by Peter Gabriel originates from the idea of *interactivity*—"Interactivity is exciting because it helps us not just to be artists but to provide a lot of material for the audience to participate in, so that eventually they become the artists themselves and can use what we create, in a sense as collage material, as stuff to explore and learn about from the inside." The *just a musician* can be thought of as kind a lecturer—a one-way presentation of music not unlike television broadcasting. An experience designer, however, is a partner in a shared dialogue—a more than one-way presentation of the music. Interactivity is a defining feature in the transition from being *just a musician* to *an experience designer.*

> **Interactivity in learning refers to the quality of action we are able to bring to people, places and things.**

Interactivity in learning refers to three basic elements: a) people; b) places; and c) things. The *quality of action* brought to each of these elements defines the character and ultimately the value of the interactivity. We can interact with people, places and things in ways that are positive and beneficial or negative and unhelpful, as well as all the variations in between. When we are learning we are constantly engaged in bringing a high quality of action to the people, places and things involved in the learning process in order to explore an issue, discover a new solution, investigate a problem, create a new product, and design a strategic direction and tactical deployment. *Interactivity, then, is the human capability for bringing a high quality of action to the people, places and things in our lives.*

Learning is intimately connected with the articulation and experience of the range of interactivity outlined above. Strategic and tactical approaches to interactivity are developed further in *Part Two: Networks.* The implications of interactivity as a source of design for learning experiences are substantial. The first and most fundamental implication is that the core content of learning (i.e. knowledge, skills and attitudes) are completely embodied and enveloped by interactivity. The relationship between the learner and the content of learning is synergistic. The traditional educational assumption of standardized knowledge, skills, and attitudes is abandoned for a more dynamic and inclusive approach to knowledge building, skill acquisition, and the refinement of positive attitudes. In a technological sense, learning is not and cannot be a form of *push* technology. In a social sense, learning is not and cannot be a form of monologue.

INTERACTIVITY: THREE PRIMARY SOURCES OF DESIGN FOR LEARNING

People

Interacting with people is a primary source of design for learning. Sample interactions include:

· Dialogue, conversation, discussion
· Interviewing, questioning, answering
· Negotiation, diplomacy, rules of engagement

Goal: The learner creates primary information resources through interaction with people.

Places

Interacting with a diversity of places is a primary source of design for learning. Sample interactions include:

· Ethnography, anthropology, social and cultural investigations
· Hiking, survival, orienteering, mountaineering
· Engineering, architecture, biology

Goal: The learner creates primary information resources through interaction with places.

Things

Interacting with things is a primary source of design for learning. Sample interactions include:

· Scientific analysis, forensic investigation, surveillance
· Archaeological analysis, virtual explorations
· Artistic representations, simulations, animations

Goal: The learning creates primary information resources through interaction with things.

A common everyday experience of interactivity is *dialogue*. A dialogue cannot occur without an exchange of thoughts, ideas, opinions, perspectives, and views. This *quality of the exchange* is a defining feature of the interactivity taking place. In a literal sense, a dialogue is a highly interactive and evolving conversation that occurs between two or more people. In a more symbolic sense, a dialogue can be thought of as a highly interactive and evolving conversation across a broad range of people, places and things. A dialogue is also an integral element of the creation of lifelong and lifewide narratives. A seminal book on the importance of dialogue is William Issacs' *Dialogue and the Art of Thinking Together.* [Issacs, 1999 #92] His ideas about dialogue provide a good metaphor for thinking about interactivity in learning. Issac's key ideas include:

√   "Dialogue, as I define it, is a conversation with a center, not sides. It is a way of taking the energy of our differences and channeling it toward something that has never been created before."

√   "In essence, dialogue is a flow of meaning."

√   The three elemental levels of action in a dialogue are: a) produce coherent actions; b) create fluid structures of interaction; and c) provide wholesome space for dialogue.

To emphasize the connection, we can replace the word *dialogue* with the word *interactivity* to create the following statements: a) Interactivity is a conversation with a center, not sides; b) interactivity results in something that has never been created before; and c) interactivity is a flow of meaning. The main difference is that interactivity, as I have described in reference to people, places and things, contains a broader range of elements than what we would find in a dialogue. However, dialogue as a basic metaphor for interactivity is quite useful in capturing the essence of the word.

Education is a monologue with a number of predefined sides and a lack of center. It is a monologue because the source of design originates in curriculum design, or something outside of the experiences of the learners themselves. It is possible for dialogue to occur underneath the curriculum, but the fundamental orientation of the curriculum does not originate in dialogue or interactivity. This is not to say that the approach lacks utility, but it is to say that it should not be equated with learning. There is no center in education since there is really no systemic unifying fabric, such as narrative, that helps to build relationships and authentic experiences across isolated curricular experiences. We emerge from an educational experience with a particular kind of expertise that has value, but that expertise is often a discrete and limited form of experience. The reason for this is simple—the educative experience is not centered in the learner as a source of design. Training is a more specific version of the educative experience that is focused on mastery of methods and techniques. Both education and training originate in monologue and lack a sustainable center for dialogue and interactivity.

In *Pedagogy of the Oppressed,* Paulo Freire coins the phrase a *culture of silence.* The phrase refers to a state of ignorance in which a peasant is trapped in poverty without realizing the forces that placed him or her there in the first place. This condition of oppression can be caused as much by a person's education as by economic forces. As a solution, Freire constructs the idea of teaching literacy (i.e. reading, writing, speaking, listening) through a practical and interactive study of the everyday lives of the people.

> **Utilizing certain basic contradictions, we must pose this existential, concrete, present situation to the people as a problem that challenges them and requires a response—not just at the intellectual level, but also at the level of action. (Freire, Paulo 1970)**

In other words, real literacy is not merely an academic study of reading, writing, speaking and listening, but an interactive study of language to clarify private and public experiences and then to take action. The possibilities and limitations that are right in front of us can be the hardest to see. In other words, the oppressed are given a practical and concrete means to construct narratives that raise their consciousness of modern life. Silence turns to voice. Monologue turns to dialogue. Inaction turns to interactivity. Literacy under the guidance of interactivity is a flow of meaning across language and social reality.

Erik Weihenmayer centered himself in the interactive realm of dialogue. For Weihenmayer, literacy is the basis for changing the social perceptions about the abilities of blind people. Weihenmayer used the Internet to create a sense of dialogue with society while climbing Everest. When we engage in a dialogue about his story, we are really involved in a deep search and longing for ways of modeling our own lives. If we are motivated by the dialogue we may connect our lives to it by finding a way to literally or symbolically participate in a manner that makes sense.

Interactivity in learning is about improving the quality and diversity of action in our lives, and is an essential foundation for the creation and preservation of narratives. If we think of narrative as the engine of learning, then interactivity is the source of energy.

Mobility

The popular idea of *mobility* immediately invites us into the technological world of wireless communications: wireless networks, mobile phones, wireless PDA (Personal Digital Assistants), satellite communications, and radio. These tools are considered to be mobile since they do not rely on a physical wire to connect the device to the communications system. People can literally carry a network in their pockets, in contrast to sitting behind a desktop computer that is immobile and dependent on physical wiring for access to the Internet. The development of mobile technologies, and therefore our own flexibility to carry our network technologies with us wherever we wish to go, is an important technological innovation for learning, education and training. Mobility will not only challenge us to master wireless technologies, but also provide critical and creative opportunities for decentralizing learning, education and training in fundamentally important ways.

Education and training are largely immobile since they predominantly take place in a centralized location. In the case of education, this is the institutional system of schools, colleges and universities. In the case of corporate training, this is the training facility or, more recently, a web server that broadcasts e-Learning content. It may seem unusual to include a web server as a physical location, especially in light of the fact that one of the promises of network technology is to deliver training anytime, anywhere. It is true to say that the physical location of the training is more distributed by virtue of the fact that it is sent to computer systems linked to the network. Nevertheless, this constitutes a single point of physical control that originates on the web server, and therefore represents a kind of physical location not unlike a classroom. The fact of the matter is that the character of the location is *not* fundamentally altered by virtue of people accessing education and training content on their office or home computer systems. In spite of all its promise, the Internet in education and training remains a highly centralized and controlled process that makes little if any use of real mobility in learning. Providing people more of the same through wireless technologies remains an amplification of familiar past practice. Laptop computer programs in many institutions are examples of this in that students have some flexibility in the places they can conduct their studies, yet what they are studying and how they are studying it is not fundamentally altered. There is currently little innovation to be found in our current use of the mobile technologies and the Internet to deliver education and training.

34

1. Narrative and Modern Life

The idea of mobility as a vehicle for cultural transportation describes the ways in which we can travel to the world, as well as the ways in which the world can travel to us.

Mobile technologies invite us to reconsider physical context and situation of learning. What this really means is that *we cannot consider mobile communications without also considering travel and transportation.* Typically, our thinking tends to default to the idea of how we can "reach out" to the world through networks from a single location. Equally important is the idea of how we "reach in" to the Internet from wherever we are. By this I am not referring to merely accessing the Internet from wherever we are, but striving to make a *contribution* through the Internet from wherever we are. In concrete terms, mobile technologies allow us to create, access and contribute to a unified learning environment regardless of where we are in time and place. With respect to experience design, this is an important emergent property of networks for learning and will fundamentally alter the design paradigm of e-Learning.

Does this mean that a centralized physical location will no longer be of importance? Of course not, but the way in which we think about and organize centralized locations for learning will be different. The most dramatic impact and challenge will not be in the use of technology, but the ways in which mobility and networks allow us to reconsider our use of time and space. The assembly line information timetable linked to rooms and subject expertise becomes increasingly irrelevant under the pressure of mobility. The ability for the learning organization to create both a communications and transportation hub will be critical. Learning demands authentic situations and contexts, and if these situations and contexts are not available through physical transportation, then mobile communications are required to create the closest possible proximity to the experience itself. This organizational restructuring will replace the default notion of current and relevant information resources as primary resources and reposition them properly as secondary resources in learning, education and training. From an administrative perspective this may incorrectly seem like an ode to anarchy in organizational design (roles, responsibilities, scheduling, allocation of resources, etc.), but is in fact a direct path to creating stability, durability, sustainability and consistency.

Mobility, in its most powerful sense, refers to the ways in which both communication and transportation technologies can be inte-

> **grated and unified into worldwide systems of learning that are freely flowing between authentic and virtual domains.**

A workforce is considered to be mobile if the physical location of the work to be done is flexible, but the connection to the workflow process is stable. Similarly, a learning force can be considered mobile if the physical location of the learning is flexible, but the connection to the learning flow process is stable. If the workflow process or learning flow process originates from past practice, then the result is that we do exactly the same as we have done before in a greater variety of places. This is why the idea of mobility as wireless technology alone is not enough to promote meaningful innovation and change. With respect to experience design, we also need to refer back to the two other critical elements in learning: a) the primary role of narrative; and b) a deep and wide perspective on the fundamental importance of interactivity in learning. *The purpose of mobility then is to facilitate the exploration, investigation, and discovery of experiences across a diversity of time periods and locations in order to increase the quality of interactivity in learning and deepen the value of the narrative.*

Mobility results in a new set of characteristics in our institutions and organizations, for example: a) a school as a center for cultural innovation rather than a mirror of cultural traditions; b) a university as a communications and transportation hub for distributed research rather than a source of lectures; or c) a corporation as an investment in human development rather than merely brand development. The three examples above are a basis for innovation and change. The problem, however, is that we often delude ourselves into believing, for example, that the mere presence of mobile technologies must mean that the users of that technology are somehow more mobile in their work. For the most part, what really happens is that people can now accomplish the same old things in a different setting. This vision of mobility is extremely limiting and fails to capture the true potential for the holistic renovation required to make learning mobile.

> **Mobility in learning is an area of great potential and one that will cause fundamental challenges to existing norms and organizational structures. Without a deep understanding of the systemic implications of mobility, however, there is a danger of using mobile technologies to do more of the same in more places.**

Unless we are able to imagine new systemic approaches, rather than vacillating over new technological approaches and additions, we will confine ourselves to the language of innovation as variation on existing themes. There is no promise in any purported technological innovations that are inconsiderate of the larger, systemic view.

The vast majority of the technology sector originates in the grammar of the technophile. The approach here is to elevate technological innovations to the language of a human value proposition. In other words, we are made promises about the human benefits of technology that are quite often hopelessly misguided and in some cases quite foolish. Further, the language used to describe these values propositions and benefits is simple-mindedly shrouded in marketing metaphors in a kind of semantic masturbation. Since the quantity of information lying behind all this is often substantial and time consuming, we find ourselves without the opportunity to decode the real value behind the promise. Until the corporation elevates itself to something more important and profound than brand enculturation and superficial marketing campaigns, the language of the technology sector will remain nothing more than a propagandistic minefield.

Mount Everest is not a place that many of us will ever physically surmount. For Erik Weihenmayer, however, it was a place that he physically achieved and used mobile technologies to help create a greater sense of proximity between us and him. In other words, he "reached in" to the Internet in order to contribute his experience more closely to ours. We, in turn, "reached out" through the Internet in a kind of virtual handshake. We were never literally "there," but we were a lot closer to "there" than reading about it in newspapers and magazines and watching reports on television. This is an example of how another person's "field trip" can be virtually extended to us. There are many examples of this emergent trend on the Internet, but in the end, it is not only our ability to access these experiences of others but also for everyone to be able to contribute their own.

The future of mobility is not in the mass acquisition of wireless Internet technologies that we can wear as if they were a new kind of skin, but in making our minds, bodies and spirits more mobile. Clearly, wireless technologies have an important role to play within a larger and systemic view of learning, but they are not in themselves a useful foundation for innovation and growth. The narrative of Erik Weihenmayer is something far more profound and important than the already brilliant achievement of standing at the summit of Everest. To imitate Peter Gabriel's comment, he is in fact not just a mountain climber, but an experience designer. There is a story of a person's life here that transcends the innovative uses of technology to make his experience more mobile. There is an interactive dimension focused on the correction of a misguided social perception that blind people are somehow disabled. In fact, Erik is not really disabled at all, his sensory apparatus is tuned to the world in a way that sighted people cannot hope to attain. Erik's mind, body and spirit demonstrate an exemplary kind of mobility. If I am making Erik Weihenmayer sound heroic, that is fine. He is a hero in the mythical sense of the term and is therefore elemental to learning.

Mobility in learning leads to greater participation in and proximity to authentic issues and events. It emanates from the need for real and virtual transportation. The narrative of Erik Weihenmayer is an exemplar of stability, interactivity and mobility.

It is not difficult to discover exemplars of mobility. In Friere's "culture of silence" (Freire, Paulo 1970) we could also say that the teaching of literacy integrated with the social participation and improvement of the impoverished was a way of giving these people more mobility in their own society. If literacy had been taught out of context, as an end unto itself, it is doubtful that social mobility would have been fostered. In Peter Gabriel's Witness Program (see www.witness.org), the issues surrounding human rights violations in our world are given greater psychological mobility by virtue of video recording technologies and the Internet. Mobility is an important strategy for gaining a closer sense of proximity to the authentic source of the experience. Erik Weihenmayer's use of mobility is designed to leverage network communications in order to create a dialogue about the false assumptions surrounding the blind.

> *A key strategic direction for the improvement of public learning systems is the illumination and mobilization of these cultures of silence. While we may not be physically impoverished, we are definitely intellectually impoverished when we are forced to remain immobile in the face of an imposed system of thought.*

One of the negative effects of networked technology is that it has increased an existing tendency toward immobility. If we think of the wide range of transportation technologies in reference to education we see immediately that we use very little of it to help educate people. For the most part, students spend years in classrooms that look quite similar to each other. They are in many ways geographically immobile. Networked computer systems have intensified this decline in physical mobility by virtue of the fact that more and more time is spent sitting in front of a computer, and therefore less time is spent being in other situations and contexts. *This is a serious and fundamental mistake in the use of computers.* Learning is not improved by spending increased amounts of time behind a computer without a correlating increase in the amounts of time spent in different environments. What a person puts into a computer is only the result of the depth and breadth of experience they are able to bring to the computer in the first place. Like the television addict we refer to as the "couch potato," the classroom addict is a "blackboard potato" and the computer addict is a "screen potato." Mobility, whether supported by wireless technologies or not, demands that we get up off our behinds so we can literally transport the grey matter in our heads to different places.

> **The banner of "access to the Internet for all" is another clear example of a counter-productive trend toward immobility.**

The problem is not a lack of opportunity or potential, but an intellectual immobility in our orientations to curriculum. The bureaucratic design and structure of educational and training institutions often consciously limit, if not eliminate, the possibility for variety in the geographic and therefore intellectual environments for learning. Access gives rise to greater dissemination of the same courses and content. Improving access in the digital divide is not unimportant, but once access has been achieved we will be left with the much more challenging job of improving what people actually do with it. Access can also be thought of in terms of authentic experience, or clarifying the ways in which people are given opportunities to learn through authentic experiences. Part of this access equation is related to transportation technologies and how we can improve the ways in which we physically move people to different geographic locations. Another part of this access equation is related to communication technologies and how we can improve the ways in which we electronically move people into closer proximity to authentic experience. Left to our current conceptions of curriculum and instruction, however, the idea of access will in fact limit, if not eliminate, a more common sense and transformative approach to mobility in learning.

Strategic Directions: Narrative

ELIMINATE THE DOMINANCE OF INFORMATION TYPOLOGIES

Our vast repertoire of information (subject disciplines, subject expertise, and departments of subject disciplines) is secondary to the development of a vast repertoire of narratives that originate in the lives of people.

PROMOTE THE ROLE OF NARRATIVE AS A DESIGN TOOL

The narrative is the new source of design for learning. Information as it exists in subject disciplines, expertise, and departments becomes a raw material that is adapted and evolved in response to supporting a deeper understanding of the narratives from a wide variety of perspectives. Information is never presented outside the presence of a guiding narrative.

PROMOTE THE DEVELOPMENT OF PUBLIC AND PRIVATE IDENTITY

The narrative is the most stable and consistent reference point for learning. People are constantly searching for identity when they learn. Information, by way of contrast, is the most volatile and inconsistent reference point for learning and tends to fragment and isolate our critical and creative vitality. The only meaningful interface with information is through the reality of people's lives.

PROMOTE DIVERSITY WITHIN UNITY, ELIMINATE DIVERSITY WITHIN UNIFORMITY

A universal form of preparation for society is promoting a diversity of critical and creative vitality through the unity and guidance of the narrative. A broad conception of stability, interactivity, and mobility directly challenges bureaucratic and mechanical approaches to organizational design in learning.

COLLECT AND DISSEMINATE EXEMPLARY NARRATIVES OF PEOPLE'S EXPERIENCES IN LIFE

At the summit of its use, a narrative is the means to build coherent connections and relationships over time and location. For example, the narrative that forms the evolution of government policies and initiatives; the narrative that forms the evolution of corporate activities; the narrative that forms educational progress, and the narrative that reveals cultural innovation over time. These are all acts of synthesis and have a completely different orientation to information than our current analytical and reductionist approaches.

2. CRITICAL VITALITY

Critical vitality is a cluster of thinking styles and events that are designed to clarify our current situations and circumstances so that a new foundation for growth, improvement and innovation can be established. The purpose of critical vitality is to clarify the underlying assumptions, tacit conditions, habits, and traditions that define the structure and therefore the experiences in our lives.

> *"Who will value my ideas (methods, rules, policies, organizations, systems, etc.) and how can I communicate this value to them in a rational manner?"*

> *"Whose ideas (methods, rules, policies, organizations, systems, etc.) are these and how can I determine what value they really have to me?"*

Critical vitality is the synthesis of critical thinking and critical action. It represents a fundamental source of energy for the construction and preservation of the narratives that guide our private and public lives.

Chapter Design

Critical Competencies
A competency is a transient and temporary technique or method that people master in order to complete a task or activity. Competencies are external demands required to successfully negotiate a work flow process, a rule, or the use of a tool.

Critical Capacities
A capacity refers to the optimum conditions, requirements, or opportunities for the development of human potential. The development of human capacities are inexorably linked to the context or environment in which people are required to perform.

Critical Capabilities
A capability is a shared human interest and need that leads to clear and concrete improvement in local, regional, national and global spheres. In this realm, critical vitality is aimed at questioning the source of control, structure, and power in our world.

Critical vitality is essential to learning.

The word *critical* refers to our ability to judge, evaluate, and assess the situations and circumstances in which we find ourselves. Vitality is the energy required to sustain growth. In other words, the idea of being "critical" does not merely mean to make a negative judgment or to find fault. This is a necessary aspect of critical thinking, but is not the final objective.

Critical vitality in learning directly challenges underlying assumptions, biases, and tacit effects in order to *build a new foundation for private and public growth.*

The content for critical vitality is the narrative and modern life which compels us to forge practical links between our thoughts, ideas, and feelings and the reality of our present-day circumstances and situations. Abstract intellectual thinking exercises have very little value in the application of critical vitality to our private and public narratives. Disconnected sets of thinking tools develop expertise in the use of disconnected sets of thinking tools.

Critical vitality is an area of human performance that exists in the interplay between our private and our public narratives. As a private animating force, critical vitality is a constant dialogue and source of reflection with our interior world (what we know, how we came to know it, and how we value it). As a public animating force, critical vitality is a means to establish shared assumptions, foundations, and premises.

Thinking about education and training through critical vitality is a means to illuminate a number of underlying issues and problems in current practice. The most fundamental issue is the lack of connection between the abstract and disconnected sets of knowledge, skills, and attitudes we acquire through teaching, and the application of narrative, interactivity, and mobility in the rich and vibrant confluence of modern life. This cannot be effectively achieved without increasing the degree of transparency between our own private thoughts and the public sea of thought.

One strategic direction for critical vitality is in building a sense of equilibrium between private reflection and public practice. If the public world dominates the private experience, then the individual feels imposed upon and quite rightly lacks a sense of commitment and ownership in learning. If the private world dominates the public experience, then there is a lack of cohesion and unity in our social fabric since our actions are held captive to individual needs and whims. An individual will produce viable learning opportunities that emanate from their private world just as much as society will produce viable learning opportunities that emanate from the public world. An individual on their own is capable of producing results that groups could not; a group is also capable of producing results that an individual could not. It is completely false to assume that a group of people will always produce ideas and results that are of higher quality or of greater depth than an individual.

The purpose of critical vitality is to question and investigate tradition, assumptions, tacit effects, and the *silent language*. In other words we not only learn to pose questions, but also learn to *question the question* itself:

√   Whose question is this and what are their reasons and purposes for asking it?

√   Is it the right question to ask and why should I believe it is important?

√   What are the underlying assumptions and biases in this question?

√   Does the question begin to move me along a certain line of thinking, and why should I believe that line of thinking is the right one?

√   What are the most critical questions to ask and how do I create them?

The ability to ask the "right" questions, or to ask powerful questions, is the most basic means to set critical vitality in motion. The art and science of questioning is inexorably linked to the creation of deep and authentic narratives. Interestingly enough, young children have a tendency to ask powerful questions, or those questions to which we as adults tend apply diversionary tactics. Over the course of a child's education, however, fewer and fewer questions are asked. What was once an almost intuitive and natural capability seems to dissolve under the pressure of imposed information systems. Further, people in positions of authority often retreat from difficult questions since their leadership may become a little too transparent. When we return as adults to asking deep and powerful questions, we find ourselves in what feels like a new kind of territory. However, like riding a bike, once you have gained your balance, it does not take too long to get it back.

There are three ideas that provide a framework for the development of critical vitality in people: a) human capabilities; b) human capacities; and c) human competencies. The use of the word *human* emphasizes and exaggerates the obvious reality that critical thought is something uniquely human. The ideas of capabilities, capacities, and competencies are a good framework for refining a number of issues related to learning, education, and training, including aims, goals, objectives, preparation for the workforce, preparation for citizenship, assessment, and evaluation. A great deal of influence in modern day society emanates from economic change and the resulting workforce requirements, so I have decided to use this as key reference. The idea for using capabilities, capacities, and competencies is a means to create a greater sense of cohesion across our experiences.

Capabilities
A capability is a shared human interest and need that leads to clear and concrete improvement in local, regional, national, and global spheres.

Capacities
A capacity refers to the optimum conditions, requirements, or opportunities for the development of human potential.

Competencies
A competency refers to specific methods, techniques and skills that are required for the efficient completion of well-defined tasks and activities.

In a communiqué from the education ministers of the Organization for Economic Co-operation and Development (OECD) entitled *Investing in Competencies for All* (http://www.oecd.org/els/Ministerial/) an international team of education ministers focused on the idea that "Competence building for all is essential in a knowledge-based society." (OECD 2001) The report defines a competency as a general range of "knowledge, skills, attitudes, and values" pertinent to the "knowledge-based society." The report is an exercise in speculation, a list of uncertain needs, and concludes that "it is not easy to identify with sufficient certainty the new competencies needed." There is no indication of what a "knowledge-based society" might be nor does the word "intelligence" appear in the report. There are, however, consistent references to "technology." *The report asks the wrong question and therefore proceeds from the wrong premise.* The more fundamental question is, "How do we help people develop the capabilities, capacities, and competencies to be successful in the confluence of modern life?"

While having some utility, the idea of *competencies for all* is not rich enough for the development of useful approaches to career success. In other words, the assumption of acquiring competencies as a means to success is not an end unto itself. Therefore, the premise of building a perspective on "competencies for all" is inadequate. *Competencies are the lowest level of critical vitality.*

What are the optimum learning opportunities and conditions people need in order to live creative, fulfilling, and productive lives?

The word *core* is commonly used to characterize capabilities, capacities, and competencies; we hear the phrases *core capabilities, core capacities,* and *core competencies.* The word *core* serves to intensify the sense of importance by characterizing them as being primary and essential. There is a great deal of value in pursuing the ideal of exploring, identifying, and systematizing human potential and development that is core. The common problem with the phrase *core competencies* is that the nature of the competencies too often emanate from information technology rather than human potential. In other words, people are taught to perform the requirements for mastering routine processes demanded by technology but are often not taught how to move beyond this robotic-like use. The question often implicit in discussions of core competencies is, "What are the most important kinds of knowledge and skills for people to have in order to be productive (i.e. simultaneously employable, career-focused, and in pursuit of their vocation) members of society?"

Critical Competencies

A competency refers to specific methods, techniques and skills that are required for the efficient completion of well defined tasks and activities.

A competent person is someone that is adequately or suitably skilled to complete a specified task or activity in an efficient manner. The task commonly has well-defined routines and procedures associated with it. In mathematics, for example, completing a long division question involves a specific pattern of routines in order to arrive at an answer. Any deviation from the routine will result in an incorrect answer. The idea of skill in this sense is closely related to the ability to repeat these routines. Efficiency refers to repetition of the routines in the least amount of time with a minimal amount of error. From my own education I can recall the daily "Speed and Accuracy" tests in which a variety of arithmetic questions were presented with the goal of getting as many questions right in the least amount of time possible. *It is entirely possible to become quite efficient at these kinds of skills without ever needing to understand what is really happening.* In other words, a mathematics question can be successfully completed without understanding the mathematics behind it. The idea of mathematical competency does not necessarily require a person to understand what it is they are doing.

Competencies are very closely aligned with the routines and procedures required for the mastery of information technology. A well-defined body of information, whether it is mathematics, science, music or any other topic, provides a frame of reference for the development and delivery of competencies. The reasons for this are: a) the body of information is static; b) a static body of information lends itself well to analysis and reduction into components; c) a static body of information lends itself well to the development of the sequential delivery of parts or subtopics; d) a static body of information is repeatable and therefore lends itself well to performance improvement, speed and automation; and e) a static body of information provides a convenient framework for instructional design and evaluation.

Competencies reside within the *primacy of information*—when information becomes the source of designing experiences for learning, education, and training. Computer technology is essentially a mathematical embodiment of information theory. The source of design for software and hardware originates in mathematical efficiency, routines, repetition, speed, and accuracy. Becoming competent in the use of a computer means to become skilled and efficient with a specific kind of mathematical information theory, regardless of how "un-mathematical" the graphic user interface may seem to us. *Competence in the use of a computer, like the performance of a long division question, does not necessarily mean the person understands what they are doing or what is really happening.* The challenge then is to place competencies into a more meaningful and durable framework that acknowledges the importance of computer competency underneath a larger purpose. Before exploring this further, it is worth elaborating a range of problems associated with ideas such as competency, information, automation, performance improvement, reductionism, and mechanization in education and training.

The idea of education as a means to memorize and repeat facts efficiently (i.e. rote learning) is a recurring theme in education. Competency often means to acquire the mental and physical routines that automate our mind and bodies in order to accelerate the recall of the right facts and the application of the required procedures and techniques. The intent of this is to make people more *informed* and therefore *prepared for* their graduation into society, and more specifically the workplace. Performance improvement under the primacy of information means to remember the right information at the right time and to complete the right procedures in the least amount of time.

> *Now, what I want is Facts. Teach these boys and girls nothing but Facts. Facts alone are wanted in life. Plant nothing else, and root out everything else. You can only form the minds of reasoning animals upon Facts: nothing else will ever be of any service to them. This is the principle on which I bring up my own children, and this is the principle on which I bring up these children. Stick to Facts, sir! (Dickens, Charles 1854)*

Dickens challenged the transference of the industrial age mindset to the education system. His caustic association of education to industry in *Hard Times* helps to isolate and magnify the primacy of information in an extreme state. Dickens' main point—that acquiring information does not lead to education—is an echo of our past, a magnification of our present, as well as a concern for our future. In other words, *Hard Times* is a continuation of an ongoing dialogue about our relationship with information. This confusion between information and learning, education and training is no less apparent in our present day, "Information is abundant but without any fixed center around which to organize it. Our task is to hold on to the anchor of our own experience to find meaning in the sea of information." (Heim, Michael 1993) A great deal of what we are doing with new technologies, notably in the emerging field of performance improvement (and especially in the industry of EPSS—Electronic Performance Support Systems) is to find ways of organizing the sea of information, with a near complete disregard for finding a *fixed center* on the *anchor of our own experience*. The reasons for this originate in the mindset of human performance as a form of *digital hard times*.

The Industrial Revolution was a quest for machine efficiency to drive economic performance. The machine moves our thinking about performance toward efficiency. Since machines accelerate the production of goods beyond what is humanly capable, speed becomes an important defining feature of competence. In other words we embrace a completely false assumption that the faster we are able to do something with the fewest errors, the better it must be. If the goal is the mass production of material goods regardless of the value and contribution to society then this is true. Machines also reduce the cost of production in comparison with human labor. Reduced spending and increased efficiency lead to higher profit margins. The machine is also an answer to increasing market demands for products thereby increasing scale of production. Under the machine, competency becomes closely aligned with efficiency, that is, increased speed, scale, and repetition of performance and a decreased cost of performance.

Machines are worshipped because they are beautiful and valued because they confer power; they are hated because they are hideous and loathed because they impose slavery. (Russell, Bertrand 1928)

With respect to education and training, the machine mindset produces a number of conflicts and problems. Machines can infect people with automatism, not only in the tasks they are required to perform, but also in the ways that they think (or, more appropriately, the ways in which they are not encouraged to think), and in their lifestyles. On an assembly line tasks are repetitive, routine, and isolated. The early iteration of the machine age focused on the industry of the body, the information age is focused on the industry of the mind. Automation is pervasive in both contexts. On an assembly line workers were required to perform habitual movements of their body in order to complete a given task. On an information line workers are required to perform habitual movements of their mind in order to complete a given task. *The assembly line worker built things like cars. The information line worker builds things like web pages and documents.*

Questioning the source and clarifying the problem of automatism in learning is a fundamental task for critical vitality. It is not pessimistic nor an exaggeration to say that our thinking about education and training is still dominated by mechanization and automation. Efficiency in performance when it becomes synonymous with quickly and accurately completing given information-based activities and tasks is not a foundation for learning. The idea of an Electronic Performance Support Systems (EPSS: http://www.epss.com/) is largely an example of the Industrial Age assembly line being retrieved and mimicked through digital technologies. "EPSSs are sets of tools that effectively automate training, documentation, and phone support, integrate this automation into applications, and provide support that's faster, cheaper, and more effective than the traditional methods." (Marion, Craig 1998) When efficiency is equated with reduced operational costs for corporations, it is only natural that performance and cost efficiency become aligned. This is a completely irrelevant strategy for learning.

The idea of teaching people to *question the source* is a well-known principle for improving the awareness of the world around them. A comment from Justin Trudeau appearing in the Toronto Star newspaper captures the essence of thinking skills as a core competency in a very practical manner:

> *"Whose definition? Whose history? Why are you teaching me this? . . . Thinking—really rational, critical thought—is deeply, fundamentally, subversive. . . . I can't teach them anything about computers. But I can teach them to think . . . to ask the tough questions of media, of corporations, of industry. Not to attack authority but to investigate it, understand it." (DiManno, Rosie 2001)*

The art of questioning is one of the greatest resources for education experiences. Questions that go to the source are the greatest resource for critical vitality as well as being distinguished as the most feared intellectual and emotional predators since they raise the transparency of people and therefore pose a kind of threat to authority. In corporate settings, asking these kinds of questions can sometimes place the future of your employment in jeopardy if your superior uses their position to mask their own insecurity and fear. About the electronic performance support system we might ask, "Whose support system is it and why should I believe it matters?" In making a question such as this public we question and challenge the nature of the authority and expertise that has demanded it. Without these kinds of questions proliferating the educational experience, there is very little opportunity for the development of critical vitality beyond the mere resignation of accepting what is.

Critical vitality is the predator; assumptions and propaganda are the prey.

The intensification of automatism and mechanization in modern education and workplace performance is not an illusion. In the present day, mechanization is no longer a physical set of gears and levers called a *machine*, but a psychological set of gears and levers called *curriculum*. It is only natural to try and bridge the perceived benefits of mass production to mass education. We have achieved this. The curriculum is the machine of mass education designed to make learning efficient (increased speed, scale and repetition at a decreased cost). The underlying assumption is that the proven benefits of the machine in mass production are also beneficial with respect to people in mass education. The idea of competency in education is not dramatically different from competency in the *Hard Times*.

Technology is a word that refers to the processes by which people create tools and machines that are designed to increase human efficiency. *Curriculum is a technology* by virtue of the fact that it is a process for classifying information in order to automate schooling. Curriculum is a child of the printing press. Print is the medium in which curriculum is embodied. The printing press is a machine that automates the mass distribution of text. The source of design for education is not really expertise, or the subject discipline, but print technology itself.

The technology of curriculum uses our age to classify people into a numbered sequence of grades, for example, all six-year-olds will proceed to grade one. Age is a universal brand and a powerful form of automation. Another number used to identify us for record-keeping purposes is the student identification number. The more people are equated to numeric identities, the easier they can be monitored. Class size is an additional number that controls the quantity of same-aged children in a classroom. The organization of students into numeric compartments is a means to make the operations of the school system more efficient, but this should not be confused with making education more effective. The implication is that by virtue of our age we have experiences, needs and interests that are close enough in proximity to permit numeric groupings and sequences. Once we reach the age of eighteen, age no longer seems to matter and we are all classed as adult learners.

Numbers are also used to control time. The student in the school system is on a *temporal assembly line*. The school schedule is numerically compartmentalized and sequenced into specialized blocks of time. Subject disciplines (e.g. History, Language Arts, Science, etc.) are seriated into information modules.

Hours, days, weeks, and years are timetabled. Digital technology has further entrenched this temporal aberration through software designed to make the creation of timetables and schedules easier. The clock is the despot of experience. Numbers create blocks of time that are autonomous mechanical systems serving to regulate the human learning process.

Numbers are used to control *location*. In the end, schools are spreadsheets; classrooms are cells, each with its room own number and formula. The keeper of the cell is the teacher. The reality of the learner in the school system is to achieve the maximum degree of assimilation, to be judged successful by that system and therefore be prepared for entry into society. This application of number to education through age, time, and space creates a physical embodiment for education that limits and mechanizes the way we acquire and develop knowledge.

The primacy of information leads to a bureaucracy of automation, print, age, time, and location. Expertise becomes isolated and abstracted from experience and therefore develops its own unique grammar. The words and syntax used to teach the expertise of physics, mathematics, geography, and history are dramatically different from each other. In effect, language is the first and most formidable means to isolate and protect the area of expertise by undermining more connected or interdisciplinary approaches with an alphabetic mine field. In other words, education is structured and organized by funneling the real life experiences of expertise into a sea of print and automated delivery methods. What people subconsciously learn in print-based education is more about how print technology symbolizes an area of expertise and less about the experience and practice of the expertise itself. Curriculum is in this sense an alphabetic voyeurism of modern life.

From this perspective, the idea of competency in education has a close resemblance to the idea of efficiency. Competency is often founded on the increased speed, scale and repetition of performance and a decreased cost of implementation. The factory assembly line is the technological symbol of workplace competency. The printed curriculum is the technological symbol of educational competency. Both symbols—the assembly line and the curriculum—originate in the primacy of information. Understanding both the opportunities and problems of curriculum in learning, education and training is fundamental to growth.

Curriculum is in fact a form of information technology—an application of methods and tools to achieve educational objectives. Ralph Waldo Emerson describes the adverse side effects of the technologies we use to preserve facts and information:

> *The civilized man has built a coach, but has lost the use of his feet. He is supported on crutches, but lacks so much support of muscle. He has a fine Geneva watch, but he fails of the skill to tell the hour by the sun. A Greenwich nautical almanac he has, and so being sure of the information when he wants it, the man in the street does not know a star in the sky . . . His notebooks impair his memory; his libraries overload his wit; the insurance-office increases the number of accidents; and it may be a question whether machinery does not encumber; whether we have not lost by refinement some energy . . . some vigor of wild virtue. (Emerson, Ralph Waldo 1841)*

The notion, now common today, is that all technologies are a kind of bartering system. We sometimes unwarily trade human capacities for technological competencies. We have practiced the competencies of the coach, crutches, the watch, the nautical almanac, notebooks, libraries and insurance. We have traded the use of our feet, weakened our muscles, lost our sense of sun time, have developed an over-reliance on print information, decreased the strength of our memory, confused our minds, and are less safe. A technology is an extension of a human ability and we have choice in how we choose to allow ourselves be extended. The problem lies in the fact that we become too focused on the teaching of technological competencies and therefore lose parts of ourselves in the trade. This, however, is a substantial challenge since the effects of technology can be quite mysterious and illusive. McLuhan makes the most dramatic statement for understanding our relationship to our machines, "The more the data banks record about each one of us, the less we exist." (McLuhan, Marshall 1969)

A *curriculum* is commonly an answer to the question, "What should be taught?" A curriculum divides information into categories of expertise, for example, the mathematics curriculum, the science curriculum and so on. These are constructed using ideas of *scope* and *sequence* of knowledge, skills, and attitudes. Being *competent* in this environment means to acquire the routines and processes pre-determined and imposed by the subject discipline.

> *The fundamental shift required for curriculum innovation and growth originates at the level of basic assumptions. The clarifica-*

tion of core competencies in the absence of a vibrant perspective on capacities for learning, education, and training will only serve to further entrench existing practices.

The Organization for Economic Co-operation and Development (OECD) document "Investing in Competencies for All" was aimed at identifying competencies that are pertinent to the "knowledge-based economy" while at the same indicating that it is not easy to identify with any certainty what these competencies are. The first problem identified was that the assumption of a "knowledge-based economy or society" was not clarified, so the foundation from which to build competencies was absent. The natural and only possible outcome of this was that "it is not easy to identify with sufficient certainty the new competencies needed." More than being "not easy," it is in fact *impossible* under these circumstances. The source of this problem is that the group of ministers maintained an assumption of curriculum as information in the face of an imaginary or at least illusive notion of a knowledge-based economy. More simply, they were attempting to continue the Industrial age tradition of transforming modern life into a predetermined form of expertise that could be inculcated into the education system in order to prepare people for the future.

The development of core competencies cannot originate in the assumptions of past practices in the face of an imagined future.

What is the source of design for the development of core competencies? The answer to this is clear. The source of design for core competencies must emanate from a reconsideration of the basic assumptions that impose limitations on our thinking so that we may reconsider critical vitality from the perspectives of human capacities and capabilities. There are a number of important requirements in this thinking process:

√ The ideas of learning, education and training need to be distinguished from each other.

√ The tendency in our thinking to apply past practices to an imagined future or ideal needs to be replaced by a thinking process that originates in the realities of modern life, proceeds to reinvestigate past practices for value, and quite literally invents practical strategic directions and tactics for designing the future.

√ Without an ability to clarify premises and underlying assumptions, innovation and growth will always be imprisoned by the boundaries of traditional practice.

√ The shift in our premise from information as the source of design for curriculum to authentic experience as the source of design for curriculum is fundamental to the meaningful articulation of core competencies for learning, education and training.

In the end, the dissemination of core competencies has great importance. However, the dissemination of core competencies in the absence of a larger strategic framework that emanates from a clarification of human capacities and capabilities is an empty exercise.

Critical Capacities

A capacity refers to the optimum conditions, requirements, or opportunities for the development of human potential.

The idea of *capacities* is an invitation to lift the discussion out of the methods and skill sets implied by the idea of competencies into the realm of ideal conditions or opportunities for learning. In doing so, we are reconsidering a number of assumptions in our thinking as well as laying a foundation for innovation.

Courses have been carefully calculated with a view to the inclusion of all relevant information during the three or four years of undergraduate work. The results have been a systematic closing of the students' minds. . . . The capacity to break down prejudice and to maintain an open mind has been seriously weakened. (Innis, Harold)

The *systematic closing of students' minds* is a direct effect of curriculum. Innis' comment exemplifies the institutionalization of information; that is to say, the university curriculum is designed to include *all relevant information* and generally *disregards the inclusion of authentic student experiences*. This, more than anything else, creates a foundation for the mechanization and automation of people. We literally become *bored-dumb*. The primacy of information, like poverty and depression, is a form of psychological oppression. What education systems need to institutionalize is *relevance, understanding,*

54

and meaning, not knowledge, skills, and attitudes. Poverty is not only an economic reality, but is also an intellectual reality.

The capacity for print media to define the conditions, requirements, and opportunities for learning is clearly profound, but not optimum. The reason it is not optimum is that the source of curriculum does not emanate from the experience of people, but the experience of information. The degree of intermediation between genuine and authentic experiences and the print experiences is extremely wide. The capacity for people's authentic and genuine experiences to define the optimum conditions, requirements and opportunities for learning are far more profound than the capacity for information and print media to do the same. The use of print media is an important *competency*, but not a *core capacity* for critical vitality.

> **Enough is enough, I resolved. I would not be forced to play by other people's rules. (Weihenmayer, Erik 2001)**

Blind people animate their intelligence in ways that sighted people do not. Sighted people animate their intelligence in ways that blind people do not. Both are wonderful and exceptional. However, drown a blind person in the sea of information curriculum found in most systems of education and training, and we can clearly understand just how incompetent sighted people can be. Erik Weihenmayer's wonderfully describes his traumatic experiences in a school system that attempted to force him into their alphabetic version of human potential, rather than understanding the potential that was in the person. [Weihenmayer, 2001 #89, see Chapter 4: Helplessness] The primacy of information was of little practical use to Erik, however, wrestling and rock climbing were profound life-changing learning experiences that encouraged his tactile, or kinesthetic, intelligence. The fact that the school could not "modify" the curriculum to ensure Erik was successful is only an indicator of the school system's inability to see any possibilities beyond its own self-imposed rules and assumptions. *Worse, the school system often promotes a false sense of self-esteem and entitlement in people—a practice that is ultimately deeply insulting and painful.* Erik Weihenmayer's narrative is one of mythological success, but how many students with less resolve than Erik, physically challenged or not, succumb to the dictatorship of print?

Howard Gardner's description of the Reggio system of twenty-two free municipal preschools and thirteen infant daycare centers in Northern Italy is remarkable:

> *In my view, the central endeavor consists of the daily interaction among teacher, students, and sometimes parents and other adults from the community. . . . The educators of Reggio Emilia have developed and continuously improved a set of techniques for taking the ideas and actions of young children seriously . . . it is not possible to plan such a curriculum in advance. Rather, the particular reactions of particular children to particular experiences become the bedrock, the driving force of the "curriculum." (Gardner, Howard 2000)*

The source of design for the Reggio curriculum originates in the authentic experience of people, not information. Innis refers to a system of curriculum in which the source of design is print information given the name *curriculum*. Gardner describes a curriculum that originates in *the particular reactions of particular children to particular experiences*. This fundamentally transforms the meaning of the word *curriculum* by changing the underlying assumptions and premises for learning. The capacities required by the teaching staff at the Reggio are dramatically different than the capacities required to teach in an information-based curriculum. The conditions, requirements, and opportunities for learning are also completely different. The reason for this is clear—the core capacities at the Reggio originate in a vision of human potential, not information theory.

The idea of *particular reactions to particular situations* is fundamental to critical vitality. Moe Norman learned to play golf by studying the particular reactions of particular parts of his body to particular swing results. Have you ever tried to learn to golf from a book? It is a wonderful experience if the book is symbiotic with a disciplined kinesthetic and tactile approach. The image of the golf swing in print and the actual feeling a golf club is an example of the gap between print and action.

> *And then I would go home at night and think to myself about which muscles were more tired than the others. Which ones still wanted to hit another ball? How did my left eye feel compared to my right eye? Since my right leg was much more tired than my left leg that means I was keeping my weight back there too long. My body did my talking to me. My body memorized my swing. (Golfer—Moe Norman)*

The phrase *my body did the talking* reveals a grammar between the reactions of his body to the experience of swinging a golf club. This is an important insight into not only how he thought about his golf swing, but also how he

56

learned how to learn. What is revealed here is the literacy of the body swinging a golf club. Many golf instruction books are focused on identifying positions and paths for swinging a golf club in an attempt to help people better visualize and analyze their own swing. In other words, learning to swing a club through print and static images is an extension of the eyes. Norman's description clearly indicates that his process for learning to swing a club is an extension of his muscles—a kind of tactile literacy. Although Moe Norman is not blind, he clearly *saw* through his muscles more than his eyes. Howard Gardner might refer to this as *kinesthetic intelligence.* The act, experience, and feeling of swinging a golf club, like many sports, is fundamentally a tactile experience and therefore requires a literacy of touch in order to reduce the gap between how we think about swinging a golf club and the experience of swinging it.

A curriculum dominated by print media is a learning experience sentenced to alphabetic abstraction and sensory deprivation. The idea of literacy is better thought of as a capacity in learning, education, and training, and secondarily as a set of competencies.

The source of the problem is not print media itself, but the dominance of print media to the extreme that it has now become a tacit assumption in curriculum. This does not mean that *literacy* is the issue, in fact, it may be that our view of literacy as proficiency in reading and writing is too narrow. The idea of being *literate*, in the most general sense of the word, refers to the quality of being well informed and empowered to act. Paulo Friere's perspective on literacy as a context of informing and empowering people in order to overcome poverty is an indispensable model. Erik Weihenmayer's perspective on literacy as a means to empower his sense perception and "not play by other people's rules" is an indispensable model. The Reggio's perspective on literacy as a means to interpret individual and shared experiences is an indispensable model. Moe Norman's perspective on literacy as a means to read his muscles in order to develop his golf swing is an indispensable model. These four examples describe literacy not as a set of competencies (methods and techniques for learning to read and write) but as a core capacity for learning (a design on the conditions, requirements, and opportunities for being literate). Underlying each example is a change of assumption and a different source of design for thinking about learning, education and training.

The process for the development of core capacities has three basic stages:

1. **Clarify Assumptions**
   Challenge underlying assumptions through critical thinking (e.g. Harold Innis).

2. **Identify Divergent Practices**
   Find concrete and practical examples from a variety of cultural and social contexts that originate from a different set of assumptions (e.g. the Reggio, Erik Weihenmayer, Moe Norman).

3. **Invent the New Capacity**
   Define and implement the conditions, requirements, and opportunities in order to establish innovative organizational designs and practices.

The idea of the "hidden curriculum" means that there are a number of effects taking place that avoid our detection, or at least make us feel that we are unable to change them. *They can be changed*, and the first step toward making the change is to clarify the assumptions for what they are. The curriculum is a machine that forces us into leading lives of efficiency by controlling the time and our place of people through information. By this I mean that the people involved in learning, education, and training are often so externally driven by imposed responsibilities and requirements that the opportunity to clarify assumptions is difficult, if not impossible, to find. The responsibility for providing the right conditions for everyone to clarify these and other assumptions lies with the realm of government. Unfortunately, it is sad to see the amount of time, effort, and financial resources being given to secondary issues like computer hardware, software, and Internet access while the primary issues remain tacit and under-funded.

The issue and problems of assessment and evaluation provide an interesting vignette. The way in which we choose to evaluate people in learning, education and training is a constant, pervasive, underlying ground that defines and controls the assumptions of the hidden curriculum, regardless of the propaganda used to describe the visible curriculum. The Ontario Provincial Report on Achievement, 1999-2000 (EQAO 2000) identified an interesting core capacity they referred to as a *culture of assessment* in which all stakeholders in the education process would form a community of practice for the purpose of the on-going improvement of teaching and learning. The idea is a very important one.

2. Critical Vitality

However, the realization of this *culture of assessment* has the same basic problem of hidden assumptions as in the OECD's "Competencies for All." The "knowledge-age economy" and the "culture of assessment" are both ideas that are not clearly defined or articulated. The ideal of competencies for all lacks a basic foundation, making them impossible to define. The ideal of a culture of assessment is in fact a further entrenchment of provincial standardized testing and reporting. The shared problem is that they both originate in past practices and do not fundamentally question their own assumptions, even though the language used is suggestive of something new and different.

The culture of assessment as defined by the EQAO assumes that *standardized testing* and *standardized reporting practices* have fundamental value. If we bring the idea of standardized testing and the idea of culture into close proximity we immediately recognize that the two are quite different. Standardized testing originates in automation, mechanization, and the primacy of information. Culture originates in adaptation, flexibility, and the primacy of people. Since the reality of the culture of assessment lies in standardized testing and reporting, the word "culture" is misplaced. The word *culture* in this context does not refer to the totality of patterns, traits, and artifacts that are created by a community, but instead is aimed at limiting the vibrancy of the culture itself. The idea of culture leads us to consider assessment as a core capacity, or the conditions, requirements, and opportunities to promote critical and creative reflective thinking on a systemic level. The idea of standardized testing and reporting leads us into the realm of consumable information, or the methods, techniques, and skills that will go in and out of fashion over time.

The practices of standardized testing and measurement have little to do with the creation of a viable capacity for a culture of assessment.

When people's capacities for thought and action are confused with information competencies, they are reduced to numbers, grades, standardization, automation, competition, and the pass/fail malaise. In this house of cards, the report card is the joker. Tests and examinations are the data wardens for the competitive sorting and classifying of people. In a system focused on labeling people with symbols that serve as indicators of how "smart" a person is we turn learning, education, and training into a sporting event. If this were a tennis game, the learner is not a player; he or she is literally the ball.

The intended benefit of standardization lies in the idea that a minimum quality of education is distributed fairly across society so that everyone is given an equal education. The real question is what should in fact be standardized. The ideal of standardizing a *culture of assessment* as a core capacity in an education system is a very worthwhile aim, but a fundamentally different proposition from standardized testing and reporting. The idea of standardizing a minimum level of literacy for all as a core capacity in an education system is a very worthwhile aim, but a fundamentally different proposition from merely learning to read and write in the absence of a larger purpose. A culture of assessment as a core capacity would originate in the following manner:

A CULTURE OF ASSESSMENT

CLARIFY

CLARIFY ASSUMPTIONS
- Standardized testing and reporting do not facilitate the creation of a culture
- Subject disciplines and expertise are not a foundation for standardization
- Assessment is not merely an activity of reading and writing tests and reports
- Externally designed and imposed assessment leads to the isolation of the learner

IDENTIFY

IDENTIFY DIVERGENT PRACTICES
- Paulo Friere: Literacy is assessed on the ability to empower people to take social action
- Erik Weihenmayer: Imposed standards of assessment and performance became the basis for a personal revolution that was fundamental to his success
- The Reggio: The student's experience was a standardized resource for curriculum design
- Moe Norman: A highly unique and powerful model of tactile literacy and self-assessment

INVENT

INVENT NEW REQUIREMENTS
- Require the assessment of literacy to be based on social action
- Integrate and adapt to different sensory orientations in learning for all
- Institute the narrative as a means to connect the student's experience with the experience of the curriculum

2. Critical Vitality

What is more important is to develop a critical vitality that helps us to first challenge our assumptions, explore divergent examples that serve as raw materials, and invent the new conditions, requirements, and opportunities for new practices. Once a new capacity has emerged we naturally flow into creative vitality.

Critical Capabilities

A capability is a shared human interest and need that leads to clear and concrete improvement in local, regional, national, and global issues.

If an individual or organization is capable, then they are considered to possess the ability required to accomplish something. A capability is different from both a capacity and a competency. A capacity is more of an ability aimed at thinking differently in order to question assumptions and develop strategic directions. A competency is the definition of methods, skills, and techniques required to complete activities and tasks.

A *critical* capability is an ability to solve shared human interests or needs that demand immediacy. It is not difficult to identify these immediate needs, as a quick glance through a newspaper quickly reveals. The idea of a critical capability is something that very directly emanates from modern life, or the condition of our present time. In the example of the Reggio, the needs and interests of the students were a primary focus and this capacity to work in unison with the individual context is a critical capability for any education system. But the world also speaks to us from beyond our individual needs. In other words, not everything of importance emanates from within ourselves, but also comes to us from outside our own experience. Our ability to balance and integrate internal needs with external demands is fundamental to learning.

World indifferent to hunger: U.N. "There is a lot of commitment to dealing with very visible situations—like floods and people driven from their homes," he added. "The big problem is 'invisible hunger.'" He was referring to people whose everyday lives are ruined by hunger, ravaging their ability to study and work. (Star, Toronto 2001)

The eradication of world hunger is one possible critical capability for all learning. "Why is human starvation still a critical issue for over ten percent of the world's population?" According to the United Nations Food and Agriculture Organization there are 800 million people in the world that suffer from hunger. This represents a little more than 10% of the world's population. More people are currently suffering from hunger than have access to the Internet, yet more time and resources are consistently placed on expanding Internet access. Many education systems have made Internet access a priority, while the issue of world hunger is nearly invisible. The reason is that in countries where hunger is not a modern day reality in the consciousness of a culture there is a tendency not to make it a priority. The article quoted above occupies a small portion of the upper left hand corner of page fourteen in the newspaper, and is an indicator of the relative weight it is given in our own news media. In more fortunate cultures, hunger appears as largely as somebody else's issue on television or in the newspapers. We are "informed" to the degree that we know the problem is "out there." Hunger, in this sense, is reduced to a form of information that we can "participate" in largely through volunteerism and financial donations. While we may say that we are more "educated" about hunger, we have not really "learned" much about it.

The eradication of hunger in our world is a culture of assessment and a standardized test for 6.2 billion people.

The issue of world hunger is an unavoidable reality of modern life. The real "content" for learning emanates from the flow of events, problems, and issues in our world. World hunger as a personal *narrative* is different and far more powerful than world hunger as a subject discipline. If we integrate world hunger into our personal narrative it means that we have connected with it in a symbolic and mythological sense. More simply, we make part of ourselves and our personal identity through the modern day issue of world hunger. As a part of our identity, we value our own thinking and actions in relation to the authentic reality of it. Designing ways and means of *interacting* with the issue of world hunger places us in direct connection with it. Using *mobile technology* allows us an extended reach for authentic learning. Designing a learning experience in this way would force us to consider many of the societal enigmas we find ourselves in. For example:

⇒ We would be aware of the amount of violence and death that youth experience through movies and games. How many times have we seen real people really die on the screen? How many times have we symbolically vaporized the enemy in video games?

2. Critical Vitality

⇒ We would observe and possibly participate in the debate about how this affects people and what responsibilities the entertainment industry should have. We would be horrified to find that there are people that actually believe it is all harmless and the entertainment industry is blameless.

⇒ We would look at the clinical nature of schooling to see that violence and death are issues largely avoided. There is a fear of dealing with the issues of violence and death in a systemic way, regardless of the obvious fact that youth are unavoidably surrounded by it.

⇒ We would question why seeing the real death of a real person due to violence or hunger is not commonly something exposed to students. How can we ever combat the irresponsibility and predatory drive of the entertainment industry if people never connect with the reality of violence and death? What is it we are afraid of—reality?

⇒ We would search for existing programs to connect to and might consider active involvement in organizations like UNICEF, Amnesty International or The Witness Program.

⇒ We would seek opportunities and take action to bring the reality of death and violence to people in order to help them become more sensitive people free from the mind-dumbing effects of movies and games. We would teach that the reality of hunger is the death of a real person.

The end result of hunger is death. This is an unavoidable fact. If our world is so globalized, then why have we not effectively dealt with this basic universal right of all people? We have become information and knowledge zombies. It is difficult for any education system to justify not dealing directly with the issue of world hunger every year in the curriculum until the issue is eradicated. For the fortunate majority of people in the world, hunger is not an issue that emanates from personal need, but is instead an external need that other people have. Hunger is a silent assumption in most schools in that we accept that hunger exists and develop a level of empathy with it. If we imagine that one-third of the school systems in the world adopted the eradication of world hunger as a critical capability I believe we would make much more substantial progress than the existing forms of volunteerism and financial donation (n.b. which of course remain important to maintain). The potential power of linking and leveraging entire school systems from across the globe in the literacy and social activism of world hunger would be a magnificent source of change and innovation.

Strategic Directions: Critical Vitality

ELIMINATE THE FEAR OF ASKING CRITICAL QUESTIONS

People in authority need to overcome their fear of people questioning the underlying assumptions that provide them with authority and control. Everyone in an educational system should be questioning the assumptions of the education they are receiving, not to oppose authority, but to ensure that it is responsible.

ELIMINATE THE FEAR OF DEALING WITH THE REALITY OF MODERN LIFE

Too many of our educational experiences are sterilized and clinical in a weak attempt to make the learning environment psychologically and physically safe. Critical events in the world are often no more than a mere pause in the never-ending drive of the imposed curriculum. This, in fact, is illustrative of the fear of authority figures to deal with reality. Ultimately, an environment that is psychologically and physically safe is one that embraces the glaringly obvious realities in our world.

ESTABLISH NEW PREMISES FOR LEARNING, EDUCATION, AND TRAINING

The imposed curriculum and clinical forms of instructional design are the accepted norm in many systems of education. The complexity they portray in print has the effect of making them less accessible to the general public. Further, there is no evidence to suggest that tradition is the best organizational design for systems of learning.

INSTITUTE A CRITICAL VITALITY DIMENSION IN TEACHER PREPARATION

One important purpose of teacher preparation institutions is to certify teachers that are both enabled and empowered to critically challenge existing practices in responsible ways. This is the front line for critical vitality.

INSTITUTE A CRITICAL VITALITY DIMENSION FOR STUDENTS

Students should be allowed and encouraged to pursue questions such as, "Why do I need to learn this stuff anyway?" It may in fact be that they really don't need to learn it, with the exception of being told they have by the decision-makers above. These decision-makers need to be made far more accountable for the curricular impositions they force on masses of people.

2. Critical Vitality

COLLECT AND DISSEMINATE EXEMPLARY NARRATIVES OF CRITICAL VITALITY
The provision of narratives that capture and elevate the critical endeavors of specific people in specific circumstances is a replacement
for abstract models and generalizations about critical thinking processes. Critical vitality is taught through the experiences of people, not
the experience of models.

3. CREATIVE VITALITY

Creative vitality is a cluster of thinking styles and events that result in the design, construction, and expression of new contexts, situations, and circumstances. The purpose of creative vitality is to make and build structures and organizations that promote growth and innovation in practical terms. Critical vitality is the synthesis of creative thinking and creative action.

> What can I design, build and take action on in order to promote new strategic directions for personal growth?

> What can we design, build and take action on in order to promote new strategic directions for public growth?

The complete integration of both critical and creative vitality is essential in building a narrative. Without critical vitality, our narratives will wander into the abstract and disconnected representation of things (i.e. doing in the absence of thinking). Without creative vitality, our narratives will denigrate into mere armchair abstraction (i.e. thinking in the absence of doing).

Chapter Design

Creative Effectiveness
The idea of effectiveness positions creativity as a very practical and concrete approach across the entire landscape of experience. Creative thinking is not limited to aesthetics and free expression.

Creative Improvisation
Improvisation is the essence of creative vitality and a superior organizer for learning experiences. This creative capacity quite literally forces the integration of thinking and doing.

Creative Achievement
The end result of creative vitality is achievement and contribution at both a personal and a public level. The idea of achievement is inexorably connected to the quality of thought as it relates to the concrete action taken.

Creative vitality is essential to learning. The word *creative* refers to our ability to imagine, design, to make and produce, and to communicate. Vitality is the energy required to sustain growth. The idea of being *creative* does not only mean to express oneself in an aesthetically pleasing or expressive manner. This is a necessary aspect of creative thinking, but it is not the final objective. Creative vitality in learning results in the creation of new perceptions, perspectives, approaches, strategic directions, and communities of practice *in order to* implement new practices and organizations. The underlying ground for creative vitality is the confluence of modern life, which forces us to implement practical links between our thoughts, ideas, and feelings and the reality of our situations and circumstances. As a private animating force, creative vitality is a constant source of renewal, reflection, adaptation, and evolution. As a public animating force, creative vitality is a source of systemic growth.

'Creativity' can be broadly defined as the constructive utilization of the daimonic. Creativity is called forth from each one of us by the inevitable conflicts and chaos inherent in human existence; it is not limited only to artistic pursuits. (Diamond, Stephen 1996)

The current role of creative vitality in education and training is extremely limited. In an information-based program, students are not viewed as creators of information but are predominantly recipients of secondary information resources (i.e. information not created by the learner). We might perhaps agree that there is a *degree* or *modicum* of creativity within the confines of subject discipline expertise and imposed forms of assessment, but the nature of this creativity is more akin to variations on a theme. Creative vitality is a direct challenge to this practice by strategically positioning the learner as a *creator* of primary information resources, as well as a user of secondary information resources. Positioning the learner as a creator of information may result in protectionism and defensiveness of existing information practices since creative vitality shifts the locus of information control from the bureaucracy to the user. The meaning of the word *curriculum* takes on a new form; the question of *what to teach* moves away from the standardized body of information and assessment toward the creation of primary information resources (i.e. information resources created by the learner). This does *not* mean that the locus of control is completely in the hands of the learner, only that the creation of information is predominantly the responsibility of the learner.

3. Creative Vitality

Until we recognize that the learner is capable of and essential in creating information, our ability to innovate our systems of education and training will remain impaired. Embracing creative vitality in learning means that we are literally building new practices based on new sets of assumptions. The nature of control and structure changes from the desire to deliver information to the desire to coordinate networked systems of interaction that facilitate the creation of information. It is not in any way a loss of organization and structure; it is an entirely new organization and structure for learning. It is not in any way a loss of accountability and responsibility; it is an entirely new sense of accountability and responsibility. It is not in any way a transfer of power and control to the learner; it is a new locus for power and control for all participants.

Creative vitality in learning is fundamentally aimed at establishing new relationships that result in new orientations to our underlying principles of power, control, authority, organization, structure, assessment, and evaluation. If the public requirements of learning are over-generalized then the learner will face a constant struggle with finding a reason to be motivated. If the individual or private requirements of learning become too dominant, then the ability of that individual to share, collaborate, and contribute to others becomes impaired. Neither extreme is useful. An important opportunity for creative vitality lies in finding ways of creating equilibrium between the needs and requirements of the private individual and the needs and requirements of public life.

The purpose of creative vitality is to imagine, design, make, produce, take action, and communicate. In other words, it is a link between what our critical vitality informs us of and what we are going to do as a result of it. The creative learner is one that constantly seeks to take action in the face of the unknown. This significance and depth of creative vitality is grounded against fundamental ideas such as Campbell's *inevitable vale of tears*, Weihenmayer's *the moments of bliss that connect you with who you are* or Gabriel's *stuff to explore and learn about from the inside.* Creativity as a human instinct is embodied in the eternal and everyday struggle we all face between good and evil. At a simplistic level, creative vitality results in new information resources. At its most profound level, creative vitality literally results in living a creative life.

Creative Effectiveness

Creative effectiveness results in concrete products (ideas and artifacts) that provide a working basis for innovation and growth.

The human capability for creativity is one of the most powerful forces in humankind. At the same time, it is an idea that defies a neat definition and the processes involved are even more difficult to understand. This makes it an ideal candidate for learning. The notion of *creative vitality* is an idea directly aimed at kinds of creativity that are focused on building practices and organizations to support new sets of principles and assumptions. In this respect, it is a highly controversial form of creativity and one that seeks to attract conflicting views. There are a number of false assumptions about creativity that need to be immediately eliminated from our discussion here.

The first false assumption about creativity is the idea that it is merely a form of aesthetic expression. Creative effectiveness is something far more significant than this. In its deepest sense, creativity is a constant challenge to our own identity, existing practices, and traditional norms of acceptance. Creative vitality can produce emotional responses that range from the exhilaration of discovery to the trauma of discovery. The Artist, in the most authentic sense of the word, is a person that probes into the depths of human achievement and struggle. To think that creativity results in something that is merely pleasing to the sensibilities is misguided. Real creativity demands courage, risk, and facing the unknown. It is the work of heros and leaders.

A second false assumption is the idea that creativity is the unique province of the Arts. Without any question, the Arts have an essential perspective on creativity, but they are *not* the sole proprietors of creative vitality. All too frequently the Arts are taught in completely uncreative ways, forcing many students into acts of interpretation and mirroring rather than exploring authenticity and identity. The reason for this does not emanate from the Arts themselves, but from information-based curricular structures that impose facts, techniques, and methods that erroneously lay claim to walking a creative path. For example, in many music curricula the dominant form of experience is that of interpretation (i.e. learning to translate a given musical composition into a personal performance). In other words, students learn to read music in order to sing in a choir or play in a band. Musical improvisation, the most genuine creative foundation of any musical endeavor, is not the traditional norm. Therefore, while many of interpretive performances have the value of being aesthetically pleasing and may serve to build positive self-esteem and public relations, they are not exemplars of creative vitality in any meaningful way. These kinds of experiences, with respect to creative vitality, are impotent in the end.

A third false assumption is that the Arts are not core elements of the educative experience, whereas language, math and science are. Not only is this assumption utterly ignorant, it is also deeply damaging. The confusion results from the fact that the Arts, under the pressure of information-based curricula, are denigrated to interpretive routines rather than authentic discovery. Supporters of the Arts as they are currently taught fight a losing battle. Denigrators of the Arts for their potential in developing creative vitality also fight a losing battle. It is true to say that the Arts as a form of information (i.e. the interpretative act of acquiring theory, technique, methods, and skills) are not central. But this is not to say that the Arts as a means to promote authenticity and originality are not critical. For the Arts to be of value in education, interpretation must give way to the primacy of improvisation. The act of improvisation is an essential and pervasive dimension of learning. The experience of improvisation immerses people in authentic exploration and discovery.

Finally, the artificial separation between what is commonly referred to as critical thinking and creative thinking is moot. As a means to focus on various dimensions of thinking these categories are useful, as long as we never lose sight of the fact that they co-exist and are inseparable. Critical thinking involves creative dimensions; creative thinking involves critical dimensions. In practical terms, a scientist engages in creative kinds of thought as much as they do critical thought. They are a kind of artist. Similarly, an artist engages in critical kinds of thought as much as they do creative thought. They are a kind of scientist. One style of thought may be more critical than creative or vice versa, but they do not exist independently of each other.

> **The effectiveness of creative vitality originates in the improvisatory spirit. It is improvisation more than any other creative force that serves to elevate our experiences in life. Interpretive experiences and mechanized curricula are not viable foundation for creativity.**

Many corporations, governments, education systems and cultural organizations seek creativity as a means to revitalize and stabilize their own survival. A corporation seeks creativity in order to increase return on investments and profitability. A government seeks creativity in order to improve the living conditions of its constituents. An education system seeks creativity in order to improve the quality of education delivered to students. A cultural organization seeks creativity in order to facilitate the improvement of lifestyles and living conditions of people. In this sense, creative vitality is a form of intellectual capital. Those that can leverage it will survive and prosper, and those that can't may not survive and prosper.

An interesting headline appeared in a local newspaper:

> *CANADA IN CREATIVITY CRISIS: STUDY A new report says there is some truth to the notion that Canadians are a somewhat plodding and not very creative people, and suggests a traditionally Canadian approach to the problem: the establishment of a commission on creativity. (Kondro, Wayne 2001)*

The report states that Canada has "tended to be a receiver, a secondary culture." According to the National Post, the recommendations in the report include:

⇒ The creation of a *Task Force On Creativity* that would include a diverse representation of scientists, business people and artists to identify and promote a culture of creativity in Canada

⇒ Expanding the ability of people to think in a variety of ways (e.g. metaphors, empathetic thinking and imagining)

⇒ Oblige Canadian universities to create more interdisciplinary approaches to courses and research

⇒ Increase funding to speculative research projects

The hypothetical goal of the task force would be to find ways of creating an "economic, social, and cultural renaissance." A columnist to the National Post newspaper writes the next day, "Oh dear. I can't think of any metaphors this morning. I must be having a creativity crisis. That would figure, given that I'm a Canadian." (Pearson, Patricia 2001) Later on she points out that Canadians need to stop being so "neurotically imaginative about crisis," and to stop devoting "a great deal of first-rate intellectual energy to feeling insecure." A more interesting focus for this response might have focused on the question, "What does a *more creative nation* really mean and what is the real value of it?"

Creativity is often positioned as a solution to crisis. From a political or corporate perspective, a crisis is a marketing strategy designed to encourage need, desire, and want in people. Need, desire, and want become the basis for offering a creative solution—and therefore a means to make money or garner public support. The real crisis surrounding the *Canada in Creativity Crisis* dialogue is the lack of creative vitality:

√   The report is not an exemplar of creativity in itself yet purports to promote and improve the conditions for creativity in Canada. There is an assumption that a diversity of experts joining together in a common task force will result in something valuable.

√   The report confuses the idea of creative opportunity with the intensification of existing practices in education and research. Interdisciplinary practices are merely a variation on existing information themes. The root assumptions about control, power, authority, entitlement, and responsibility have not been questioned.

√   The report implies that creativity can be improved through the improvement of such thinking styles as metaphorical thinking, empathetic thinking, and imaginative thinking. Obviously the improvement of thinking is important, but thinking is only one component of the creative process and is not an end unto itself.

√   The report assumes that increased creativity commonly has beneficial results. History proves this to be incorrect.

√   The report covets taxpayer money for the illusion of an "economic, social, and cultural renaissance." The question of whose renaissance this is and why we should believe it to be of value is missing. This same problem was found in the notion of "competencies for all" described in the previous chapter.

√   The report does not make basic recommendations for the systemic improvement of learning.

It would be somewhat humorous to change the headline to, "Canada in Creativity Crisis: Even though 'Despite a substantial body of research, psychologists still have not reached a consensus on the nature of the relationship between intelligence and creativity, nor even of exactly what these constructs are.'" (Sternberg, Robert [ed.] 2000) Nevertheless, many governments market the idol of creativity as a means to resolve a perceived crisis. The invention and mass marketing of the crisis itself is the real act of creativity here and everything that follows is merely routine.

Canada is a country vibrant with creative activity and it is an obvious mistake to characterize an entire nation as being *a somewhat plodding and not very creative people.* There is no real creativity crisis, but as the report correctly suggests, finding ways of increasing creativity across the nation is a fundamental national agenda that requires a clear and deliberate strategy. The critical question is, "What do we want to be creative for?" The notion of creating an economic, social, and cultural renaissance is too vague and general—"A renaissance to do what?" We know that creativity is equally alive in criminal and violent activity as it is in welfare and human rights activism. Increasing the creative capacities of people without a guiding narrative, or fundamental purpose, might result in a cultural holocaust. If the idea of *Canada* does not exist primarily as a network of significant narratives of exemplary people, places and events in the minds of Canadians, there is no meaningful foundation for creativity.

The creative vitality of an individual, group or nation cannot be sustained unless it is referenced against something far more substantial than vague notions of "creativity" or ideals such as a "cultural renaissance." The source of creative vitality is not found in the existing practices of education, business and politics, but is found in a lifelong and lifewide understanding of the learning. It would be true to say that as a nation we have not addressed the issue of human potential and learning effectively even though we have a great deal of research and best practices developed in the field of education and training. To achieve this, we must quite literally recalibrate our assumptions and tacit beliefs, otherwise we will remain chained to innovation and creativity as a spiraling series of variations originating from the same theme. The basis for this recalibration of our assumptions and beliefs lies in the realm of *improvisation.*

Creative Improvisation

Improvisation is the natural and genuine dynamic of human creativity. We must learn to improvise, and improvise to learn.

A jazz ensemble is an artistic model of creative vitality. The source of design for the performance is found in the composer's melodic, harmonic and rhythmic structure. Rather than being an act of interpretation, however, the jazz performer's role is to create the music itself. Unity is provided by the structural elements of the composition, but the performance is never merely a literal interpretation. The jazz performer is a real-time collaborator in the composition itself. In addition, the interactive environment of the jazz performance is enriched by the real-time contribution of ideas from the other performers in the ensemble. The musical identity and narrative of the ensemble is authentically expressed each time it performs.

It is important to remember that improvisation is never merely random or chaotic. All improvisation has a focused yet liberating structure that is designed to provide unity, not uniformity. In jazz music this underlying ground is often a prescribed melody and chord pattern, but this of course does not mean that the jazz improviser will perform these exactly as written. Above this underlying ground is a sense of freedom and creativity. Each performer has the freedom to create music while at the same time being closely connected to the other performers in the group. All performers experience a form of musical confluence as they listen and respond to the musical ideas created by their co-performers. The jazz ensemble is in many ways an apt metaphor for the confluence of modern life.

A similar phenomenon can be found in folk music. Folk tunes are commonly passed on "by ear." This means of communication encouraged a greater degree of improvisational individuality and freedom in comparison with written notation. The performer was simultaneously a collaborator in the composition of the tune. The performer did not strive to repeat each note or word of a song in strict interpretation, but instead sought to convey the spirit of the song in relation to their own experiences in life.

Another interesting and important model for improvisation, again from music, is *environmental improvisation*:

Brian (Eno) set up his various gizmos, rhythm machines, toy pianos, clocks, samplers, radios, etc. and gave each musician a flash card. On it he had written a brief character description. 'You're the latest remaining survivor of a catastrophic event and you will endeavor to play in such a way as to prevent feelings of loneliness developing within yourself.' Our musicians were then enjoined to play within the parameters of those roles as was humanly possible. (David Bowie—Outside)

The improvisatory environment designed by Brian Eno in *Outside* is an excellent model of a creative *environment for learning*. By connecting each musician to a role and an emotional event Eno effectively bypasses the visual notation of musical composition and embraces a more instinctive and primordial form of expression. *Outside* is an improvised narrative that is an exemplar of creative vitality in music.

Music is the most important resource for exploring the nature of improvisation. Of course, the idea of improvisation is not confined to music. The term *bricolage* refers to an improvisatory process of making or repairing something with whatever materials happen to be at hand. A *bricoleur* is someone who completes a job by adapting whatever is at hand, usually in the absence of the required technical knowledge and specialized tools. A poorly trained and equipped mechanic attempting to fix a car is a bricoleur. We may not admire the technical capacity of this mechanic, but undoubtedly his or her thinking processes will deserve respect. An entertainment equivalent of bricolage is the television program "Junkyard Wars" in which two teams compete by making the best use of junk in a junkyard to design and construct machines that can successfully negotiate a given task. The end result is an improvised technological sporting event.

Of course, watching a broadcast of people engaging in bricolage may lead to a greater awareness, but voyeurism is not a replacement for the experience of improvisation. There may also be a number of questions about how much of this "improvised experience" is scripted behind the scenes. The increasing presence of "reality-based" television programs is *in reality* an attempt to retrieve a sense of improvisation in modern life. City TV in Toronto, Canada is notable for its location-based news broadcasts made possible by mobile broadcast technology. The Learning Channel's tag line is "Life Unscripted" and offers a series of programs that are designed to capture interesting modern life experiences in their authentic form. A popular theme in the unscripted programming genre is emergency services, including police investigation, the military, fire fighting and natural disasters—each being a window on the narrative of survival. While this closer sense of connection to "real" experience has benefit, it is still important to remember that we are all watching the same screen and listening through the same speakers. Watching people improvise is not the same as experiencing the power of improvisation.

In 1982, David Cronenberg pushed the boundaries of reality-based television to create the science fiction horror *Videodrome*. In speaking to an aggressive cable programmer through a "video letter," Professor Brian Oblivion (i.e. the Mr. Hyde version of Marshall McLuhan) describes the horrific confusion between reality and television that is the Videodrome:

> *"The television screen is the retina of the mind's I. Therefore, television is part of the physical structure of the brain. Therefore, whatever appears on the television screen emerges as raw experience for those who watch it. Therefore, television is reality, and reality is less than television." (Cronenberg, David 1982)*

In Videodrome, television is the ultimate hallucinogen. As Oblivion's daughter states in the movie, "Watching TV will help patch them (i.e. the homeless and destitute) back into the world's mixing board." The issue Cronenberg forces us to face is not the presence of "reality-based television" but the effects of *television-based reality.*

> *Asking the question, "What would curriculum and instructional design become if improvisation were used as a source of design?" is fundamental to instilling a greater sense of creative vitality in learning.*

Erik Weihenmayer is an exemplar of the power of improvisation. On one level, his blindness forced him into a survival mode that embraced creative vitality as a means to lead a full and complete life. On another level, he improvised his own system of learning in order to transcend the limitations of a highly biased and ineffectual school curriculum. Just as Brian Eno improvised the learning environment of the recording studio, Erik Weihenmayer improvised the learning environment of the mountain. They are both extraordinary bricoleurs in the sense that they find extraordinary things to do in life. Creative improvisation has three critical attributes:

Structure:
Improvisation originates from a clear structure, it is never merely random or chaotic. In music, this foundation is the melodic, harmonic, and rhythmic structure supplied by the composer. For the bricoleur, this foundation is the materials and resources immediately available to solve a problem.

Immediacy:
The improviser is in a highly collaborative and interactive relationship with the realities faced in modern life. In learning, the underlying ground of improvisation is the confluence of our experiences in modern life.

Immersion:
Improvisation is systemic. The entire range of people, places, and things immediately available in our lives are the core content for learning.

Positioning *creative improvisation* as the source of design for curriculum results in the opportunity to recalibrate the locus of control, power, authority, entitlement, and responsibility in a fundamentally new way:

THE EVOLUTION OF CURRICULUM

Improvization
1. Structure Time-centric > Lifespan centric
2. Space-centric > Lifespace centric
3. Information-centric > Identity-centric
4. Tradition-centric > Innovation-centric

Immediacy
1. Assignments, Tests, Exams > Direct Participation in Modern Issues
2. Documents and Artifacts > Direct Contribution to Modern Issues
3. Classes and Age Groupings > Teams and Ensembles
4. Information Expertise > Improvisatory Expertise

Immersion
1. Immersion Secondary Information > Primary Information
2. Information Typologies > Exemplary Human Narratives
3. Bureaucratic Planning > Interactive Planning
4. Static Experiences > Mobility of Mind, Body and Spirit

If we wish to inspire a deeper sense of creative vitality in learning, our traditional assumptions about curriculum and instruction need to be recalibrated. The path to recalibrating these assumptions is to remove information as a source of design for curriculum development and replace it with more vibrant possibilities such as improvisation.

Of course, these kinds of questions are never comfortable. The source of discomfort here would be in demoting the traditions and systems of information (i.e. subject disciplines, subject experts, systems of graduation and certification, professional development, and evaluation) to secondary resource material. Information and improvisation both have *structure*, even if the character and implications of those structures are dramatically different. The challenges of using improvisation as a foundation for the recalibration of learning, education and training for policy making, organizational design, administration, and implementation are substantial. However, the implications for not instilling a deeper sense of creative vitality in our systems of learning, education, and training are even more substantial.

Creative Achievement

Achievement is a never-ending story of individual and collective growth.

Stephen Biko (1946-1977) made a monumental contribution to our world. His is a narrative of mythic and heroic proportions. To become educated in the life of Stephen Biko may lead us into acquiring information about his life through biographical and other forms of documentation. Existing forms of expertise can be effectively leveraged to illuminate various aspects of his life (i.e. political, social, historical, technological, intellectual, spiritual, and emotional). This is of course valuable for at the very least people are given some raw intellectual materials that can be integrated with their own personal narratives. But these forms of information, however well understood, do not in themselves constitute a narrative. *The idea of Stephen Biko's life as a source of design for learning leads us into a deeper realm of experience:*

I own this cattle all right, but if someone is starting a house next door, it is custom for me to have empathy with him, it is part of my cultural heritage to set him up, so that my relationship with my property is not so highly individualistic that it seeks to destroy others. I use it to build others. (Biko, Stephen 1978)

Stephen Biko is an exemplar of an *experience designer.* He was an artist of consciousness, a designer of mass renewal, and an exemplar of lifelong and lifewide learning. His life was immersed in the structure and immediacy of apartheid. Biko's vision of an apartheid-free South Africa in the face of completely contrary forms of power and control provide an intense environment for creative vitality. Thinking about the narrative of Stephen Biko retrieves Stephen Diamond's perspective that "Creativity is called forth from each one of us by the inevitable conflicts and chaos inherent in human existence; it is not limited only to artistic pursuits." The creative environment is the *confluence of modern life.* We can now add Stephen Biko's "I use it [my property] to build others" to Joseph Campbell's *inevitable vale of tears,* Erik Weihenmayer's *the moments of bliss that connect you with who you are* and Peter Gabriel's *stuff to explore and learn about from the inside.* In the end, Stephen Biko was murdered. While the risk involved in Biko's creative vitality may be far more substantial than the majority of us will face, this example reminds us that real creative vitality is never without a degree of risk.

How can the narrative that is Stephen Biko serve as a source of design for learning? On the surface, the answer to this question is quite simple. It is *only* in the lives of people (our individual selves and others) that we can discover, explore, and acquire creative vitality. In this sense, the narrative that is Stephen Biko is not merely an historical collection of information in a book—Stephen Biko is an example of a profound life and an exemplary model of lifelong and lifewide learning. The relevance of his life holds something for us all and the potential to extend the definitive spirit and ideals of Biko is completely modern. The narrative, story, myth, and hero that synthesize to create our remembrance of Biko speak to us across the boundaries of time and cultural circumstance. There is a universality about this life that transcends historical recollection. In this sense, Stephen Biko has as much to do with our modern life experiences as the latest in current events.

> **The practical and concrete ramifications of exemplary lives to inform our own learning are profound. The ideal of lifelong learning cannot be attained without the narratives, stories, myths, and heroic deeds of exemplary people in the world.**

How do we connect a narrative that is now confined to history with the realities of modern life? The first task is to understand, as best as we can, the flow experience in Biko's life. What were his most important beliefs? What were his happiest and saddest moments in life? How did he preserve his spirit in the face of atrocities? The second task is to renew our own private identity through the lens of Biko's identity. What aspects of Biko's spirit resonate with my own? How can I expand my own beliefs through the power of Biko's life? What are the aspects of Biko's narrative that profoundly and permanently evolve my own identity? The third task is to extend this personal rejuvenation to the social sphere. What are the issues and problems in our society that could benefit from my new sense of identity and purpose?

If we return to *Canada in Creativity Crisis* and place it next to Biko's idea of *Black Consciousness* we lay a foundation for profound improvisation. In fact, Biko faced a "creativity crisis" of monumental proportions that make the description of Canada's creative crisis look inconsequential. For example, we can take three principles of Biko's *Black Consciousness* [Biko, 1978 #25] and apply them to the *Creativity Crisis in Canada*:

Psychological Renewal
To restore dignity and confidence in one's race and eliminate exclusivity of language use.

> The network dynamics of social activism designed by Biko to renew human dignity is an example of interactivity in learning. While the renewal of creativity in Canada is not aimed at apartheid, the level of conflict with existing assumptions, practices, policies, and institutions would be substantial. The dynamics of social renewal applied by Biko could are transferable.

Independence
To help people become more self-sufficient through the provision of and education in the basic tools and technologies for living.

> Biko strongly believed that education should help people to become more self-sufficient. In Biko's circumstance, this education was literally designed to assist in human survival (i.e. the provision of food, shelter, and clothing). In doing so, Biko directly challenged the existing authority and power structures. While self-sufficiency in Canada is unfortunately an issue for some, the ideas are also transferable to learning, education, and training.

Oppose Immoral Business Practices
To rally foreign powers and economic forces to build up humanity of Blacks.

> The economic isolation and resulting impoverishment of the Black Consciousness in South Africa was directly aimed at limiting their ability to

survive physically, emotionally, and intellectually. As a force of opposition in Canada, a national education system would be a formidable entity in opposing business practices that brand our culture with imagined lifestyles and materialism. Just as apartheid caused a kind of identity blindness, corporate branding also causes a kind of identity blindness.

Joseph Campbell says that our perception of ourselves and the world we are in is not adequately supported by "heroes." Biko is a hero who pursued his bliss in life in the face of the inevitable vale of tears.

It is obvious to say that the cultural time, place, and sensibilities are different between our present day circumstances and those of apartheid in South Africa. In another sense, are they really all that different? If we recall the historical treatment of the native people of Canada, the internment of Japanese Canadians, the plight of the homeless and unemployed, the imbalance of corporate power and influence, the racial tensions that exist in multicultural communities, unacceptable levels of depression and anxiety, increasing levels of gang violence and homicide, we find that the situation of Biko and aspects of the Canadian sensibility are not as removed from each other as we might like to believe. The current structure of standardized and information-based system of education and training offer little help, and may in fact be part of the problem.

> *Creativity takes us to the edge of what we know so that we may act.*

If something is *core* in *lifelong* learning or *education* then it needs to originate in narratives that provide us with practical and concrete guidance. Erik Weihenmayer and Stephen Biko *are* exemplary narratives and exemplary forms of lifelong and lifewide guidance. The essence of these narratives is not found in information, but in the spirit and purpose beyond the information. We all need to decide what actions we are going to take in our lives. Deciding what the right foundation is and taking reasonable action is essential. Creative achievement must originate in nothing less than the lives of real people in real circumstances, and therefore education can be nothing less than the celebration of heroism.

Strategic Directions: Creative Vitality

ELIMINATE THE IDEA OF CREATIVITY AS AN INFORMATION-BASED ACTIVITY

Creativity must be closely linked to a clear view of effectiveness. The raw materials for creativity are the circumstances and situations we find ourselves in, not the information we are told to learn. The idea of creativity as the aesthetic expression of information is inadequate. In fact, many things that appear to be aesthetically pleasing have little to do with real creativity.

POSITION IMPROVISATION AS A FOUNDATION FOR IMPROVING CREATIVITY IN PEOPLE

Improvisation is the most essential tool of the creative person, whether they are undertaking an artistic pursuit or not. Under the pressure of improvisation, information becomes something to be shaped and manipulated. More profoundly, our organizational design and structures become the basis for improvisation. Timetables, grade levels, assessment strategies, instructional methods and the like would all embrace the spirit of improvisation.

ELEVATE THE ARTS AS EXAMPLES OF IMPROVISATION AND CREATIVITY

Too often, the Arts are presented as if they were a form of information containing a specified set of general techniques and methods. This is a rear-view mirror perspective of the artistic sensibility that is not helpful in promoting creative vitality. The improvement of the artistic sensibilities in people is directly related to their improvisatory abilities.

COLLECT AND DISSEMINATE EXEMPLARY NARRATIVES OF CREATIVE VITALITY

The provision of narratives that capture and elevate the creative endeavors of specific people in specific circumstances is a replacement for abstract models and generalizations about creative thinking processes. Creative vitality is taught through the experiences of people, not the experience of models.

PART TWO: NETWORKS

Thought Process

A network—or the quality of connections, relationships, and associations we create across people, places, and things—is the foundation for a new approach to instructional design. The art of instructional design is synonymous with the art of creating networks.

A network learning environment is the basis for planning learning experiences. It originates in a coordinated approach to interaction design, rather than information design. There are no subject disciplines and areas of expertise that define the structure of a network learning environment. The architecture and communication of information are constantly fluid.

Learners are literally network explorers. They sharpen their skills through the living processes of exploration that surround them in such fields as journalism, entrepreneurship, entertainment, politics, and others. There is no place in learning for armchair observation.

The idea of lifework places our need for employment and our career sensibilities under the guidance of our vocation. Each of us has a kind of "calling" or intuitive sense of what it is we would like to do. Pursuing our vocation is fundamental to our success.

Probes

! *Networks replace information. Interaction replaces ignorance.*

! *A network learning environment embraces a comprehensive range of interactivity across people, places and things.*

! *Interaction design is instructional design.*

! *Learners cannot learn unless they explore. Explorers cannot explore unless they learn.*

! *To understand what our lifework should be we need to face our own death.*

Overview

Chapter 4: Network Learning Environments

Interactivity is the primary source of design for a network learning environment. A basic range of interactivity consists of an effective balance across: a) authentic experiences; b) cybersphere experiences; c) electronic media experiences; and d) print media experiences.

The Art of Instruction
Network learning environments transform the nature and requirements of instructional design. Interactivity is the new art and science of teaching. The transition from information-based design to interactive design is the foundation for network learning.

Interaction Design
The Interaction Design Matrix provides a tool for creating, planning, implementing, managing, and assessing interactivity in learning. This is the basis for reconsidering organizational design and institutional operations.

Emergence
An essential benefit of networks is that they cause opportunities and conflicts to emerge simultaneously. Understanding the real nature of the opportunities and conflicts is an important means to sustain innovation.

Chapter 5: The Network Explorers

The improvement of human ingenuity is the most fundamental aim for instructional design. By embracing the learner as a network explorer we take aim at improving the ways in which people investigate, examine, discover, invent and take action across a diversity of situations and circumstances. This is the most effective way to prepare people for the future.

Shining the Light
An instructional designer sets the stage for learning by defining the situations and circumstances for exploration. These conditions for learning are literally placed under surveillance.

Human Ingenuity
Our inventive skills, cleverness, and imagination facilitate insight into our surrounding conditions, the recognition of possibilities, the apprehension of variables, and the capacity for taking action.

Performance
Real-life examples of people engaged in exploration are the new content for learning.

Chapter 6: Lifework

Lifework is the totality of our successes and failures in the face of our own end. We will measure our satisfaction in our own lives by assessing the gap between what actually happened and what we think should have happened. Living life in a confused, reactive manner unnecessarily widens this gap.

Employability
If a person is to be considered employable, they need to possess more than transient technological skill sets. Highly intelligent people are often on the periphery of society in the sense that they do not necessarily accept the established norm and status quo.

Career Sensibility
When we face our own end, we will face the totality of our own private narrative. Since a career occupies a substantial amount of time in our lives, we cannot afford to live through careers that are less than satisfying. The value of time is far greater than the value of money.

Vocation
Lifework originates our inner calling—the things to which we are attracted in life. Each of us voices happiness, joy, satisfaction, and bliss in highly personal terms. Finding a place for this voice in society is a standardized test of universal proportion.

4. NETWORK LEARNING ENVIRONMENTS

A *network learning environment* focuses learning on the creation and strategic use of connections and relationships. It is a coordinated set of situations and circumstances for learning that empower the learner to create and evolve a range of experiences across people, places, and things. In other words, the learner

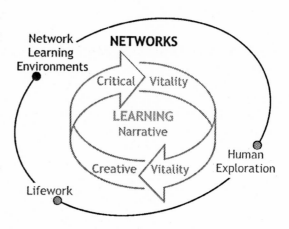

is intimately involved in shaping the learning environment to support their own motivations for learning. The means to coordinate a network learning environment is called *interaction design*.

What are the optimum conditions to support learning through networks?

A *network learning environment* requires us to reconsider the nature of power, control, authority, responsibility, and entitlement in learning. The result is not an extension of traditional classroom practices that organize learning through information typologies, but instead results in a completely different paradigm for instruction.

Chapter Design

The Art of Instruction
Network learning environments transform the nature and requirements of instructional design. Interactivity is the new art and science of teaching. The transition from information-based design to interactive design establishes the foundation for network learning.

Interaction Design
The Interaction Design Matrix provides the core tool for creating, planning, implementing, managing, and assessing interactivity in learning. This becomes the basis for reconsidering organizational design and operations.

Emergence
Networks naturally cause opportunities and conflicts to emerge simultaneously. Leveraging this conflict is the basis for capturing emergent opportunities and possibilities.

What does the phrase learning how to learn *really imply?*

The traditional answer to this question commonly focused on such notions as: the acquisition of knowledge and information in the right amount at the right time; the effective application of skills, techniques and methods to complete an activity or task independently; the ability to self-assess and self-evaluate one's own progress against performance criteria; to create personal goals, plans, and personal management systems; and the like. These notions represent the traditional rear-view mirror practice of learning how to learn. Under the influence of networks, the phrase *learning how to learn* takes on a new character.

In literal terms, the phrase *learning how to learn* is actually nonsensical. Nobody needs to "learn how to learn" since learning is in itself a universal human experience of all people everywhere. Education and training, however, are not universal experiences. Were we not learning before we learned how to learn, and if not, what were we doing? Unfortunately, the phrase *learning how to learn* is sometimes a transference of responsibility further down the educational food chain toward the student. This approach does not constitute an effective foundation for the improvement of our learning, education, and training systems.

As subcategories of learning, education and training can be thought of as organized systems of traditions and practices specific to a cultural environment. In other words, the ways in which we organize the time, space, and language of education and training defines a cultural norm and has a profound impact on the character and personality of that society. Culture itself is a learning environment that has visible and hidden dimensions and effects.

Edward Hall referred to these tacit or literally *out of awareness* conditions as *The Silent Language* of culture:

> **The fact is, however, that once people have learned to learn in a given way it is extremely hard for them to learn in any other way. This is because in the process of learning they have acquired a set of tacit conditions and assumptions in which learning is embedded. [Hall, 1959 #30 @ 47]**

This important idea has not been given enough attention with respect to the ways in which we design the cultural learning environments we call *education* and *training*. When we have *learned to learn in a given way* it can only mean that we have failed to learn in other ways.

Vibrant cultures occur in both the presence and absence of organized systems of education and training. Education and training are not prerequisites for a rich culture. Cultural identity, however, would not be possible without the phenomenon of learning. The character and style of people's learning patterns and processes result in a cultural personality. Learning cannot be contained within the walls of any education and training system; the "classroom" for learning is the entire range of situations and circumstances in which we find ourselves. Our education and training systems are for the most part psychologically closed and physically bounded by walls. The physical walls of the classroom or training facility are *not in any way* broken down by the Internet; the walls of the classroom are as sturdy as ever.

The idea of a *silent language* is related to the idea that *the medium is the message*. Marshall McLuhan proposes that technology alters the ways in which we perceive experience, think about experience, and take action. Like culture, technologies have visible and hidden dimensions:

> **Environments are invisible. Their ground rules, pervasive structure, and overall patterns elude easy perception. (McLuhan, Marshall and Quentin Fiore 1967)**

The information we communicate through media is embodied and stylized by the tools we use. The understanding and meaning we create are intimately tied to the ways in which the media environment captures and guides our perceptions, thoughts and actions. In other words, technology stylizes the learning process in a manner that is often indiscernible and unconscious. The tools we use—physically, intellectually, technologically, emotionally, spiritually—directly characterize the understanding and meaning we create for ourselves.

> **The new art of instructional design positions the quality and character of the learning environment as a shared and collaborative source of design. The object of instructional design is interactivity itself, or the systems of thought, communication, and action that are learning. The age of information-based instructional design is no longer relevant.**

If we are to improve and expand upon the *ways we are able to learn*, we must be completely focused on the creation of *diversity* in the situations, circumstances, and contexts into which we invite people. To build diversity in a learning environment means continually to offer new intellectual, emotional, and physical spaces, places, and locations for learning. People respond to different situations and circumstances in different ways. The reason for this is not the information in their heads, but the context they are in. Information may play a role in people's reactions, but it is not the source of the reaction. The information used in learning is embodied by the environment in which we find ourselves. For example, the instructional design parameters of subjects such as language, math, science, music, etc., are all uniformly bounded by a single inflexible learning environment of classrooms and timetables. Often, a great deal of attention is given to presenting information that is current, relevant, and valued, however, little if any attention is given to the environment in which the information is presented. If the environment remains the same over long periods of time, then we are in fact conditioning the way in which people learn through a form of sensory deprivation.

The Art of Instruction

A clear focus on the improvement and expansion of the *ways we are able to learn* leads toward a direct and intimate consideration of the quality and character of instructional design. The classroom is the symbol of a traditional learning environment. In a classroom, specific kinds of interactivity take place between the teacher and his or her students. This interactivity is guided by the aims and objectives of information-based curriculum resulting in relationships such as lectures, lessons, courses, and programs. The effectiveness of a classroom learning environment is validated through assessment and evaluation practices that are designed to check whether or not the students have understood the information presented in the curriculum. The fundamental building blocks of interactivity—the control of time and location—are typically not elements that can be manipulated by students. To a limited degree, the students exercise a modicum of choice in terms of the kinds of projects and activities they might select in order to "learn" the required information.

Interactivity is clearly alive and well in the traditional education and training paradigms. However, the uniform and repetitious character of that interactivity serves to limit the possibilities for learning. The reason for this returns us to an earlier probe: information-based curricula and bureaucratic organizational structures are not an effective source of design for learning.

> *A more important question is, "How can we develop more effective environments that improve and expand opportunities for learning?" This is a question of access in its most fundamental terms. In other words, a network learning environment is not as much about access to the Internet as it is access to possibilities for learning.*

The solution to this age-old dilemma is to establish a completely new way of thinking about curriculum and instructional design. The rationale for this originates in Edward Hall's comment, ". . . once people have learned to learn in a given way it is extremely hard for them to learn in any other way . . ." The *given way* in our present day is a direct reference to the information uniformity imposed on people over long periods of time. Changing the information within this uniform system of programs, courses, subjects, assignments, and tests does not alter the *invisible elements* of the environment itself. Just as the idea of curriculum must necessarily evolve from information to narrative, the art of instruction must also evolve away from uniform learning environments toward diversity in learning environments. The fundamental and most effective way to achieve this is to build a paradigm of instructional design that originates in a vibrant and comprehensive vision of interactivity.

> *Once, out for a walk across the racecourse, I myself saw people doing all sorts of things there, piping, dancing, one giving a show, one reciting a poem, one singing, one reading a story or fable, and not one of them preventing anyone else from his own particular business. (Dion Chrysostom, 70 AD)*

The phrase *and not one of them preventing anyone else from his own particular business* has a charm and a sense of freedom to it. It is a wonderful description of interactivity in everyday life. Let's imagine for a moment that we transform this description into the traditional information-based curriculum approach. A curriculum designer would first categorize this experience into courses of study such as *Piping, Dancing, Giving a Show, Reciting Poetry, Singing,* and *Reading a Story or Fable.* One would hope that *Walking Across the Racecourse 101* would not become a course of study. The knowledge, skills and attitudes required to be "educated" about this experience would have a specific scope and sequence applied to them. Students would be assessed through written tests. Oddly enough, this experience might be "taught" to students without ever having them involved in an authentic situation. It is disheartening to see the number of things that are purported to be "taught" in education and training systems without ever having students involved in experiences beyond what they see in print.

The idea of *interactivity* is far more powerful than the idea of *information*. In *Experience and Education,* John Dewey describes the *principle of interaction*:

> **The principle of interaction makes it clear that failure of adaptation of material to needs and capacities of individuals may cause an experience to be non-educative quite as much as failure of an individual to adapt himself to the material. (Dewey, John 1938)**

Interactivity, not information delivery, is the core capability for instructional design. The information argument is moot; it does not matter if the field of information in the environment is current and relevant, or even out of date and irrelevant. The *currency* and *relevancy* of information is determined by the field of interactivity that surrounds it. Nor is the environment substantively improved by virtue of the fact of high speed networks, one-to-one computer to student ratios, and pervasive access to the Internet, since a great deal of our current use of these technologies originates in information theory rather than human experience. The design of the learning environment must originate primarily in consideration of the field of interactivity, and secondarily in the field of information.

To fully appreciate this change, it is useful to illuminate the hidden assumptions that influence our current practices:

HIDDEN ASSUMPTIONS OF INSTRUCTIONAL DESIGN

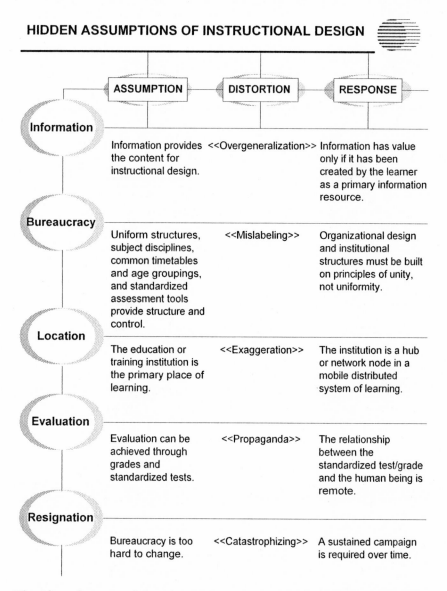

	ASSUMPTION	DISTORTION	RESPONSE
Information	Information provides the content for instructional design.	<<Overgeneralization>>	Information has value only if it has been created by the learner as a primary information resource.
Bureaucracy	Uniform structures, subject disciplines, common timetables and age groupings, and standardized assessment tools provide structure and control.	<<Mislabeling>>	Organizational design and institutional structures must be built on principles of unity, not uniformity.
Location	The education or training institution is the primary place of learning.	<<Exaggeration>>	The institution is a hub or network node in a mobile distributed system of learning.
Evaluation	Evaluation can be achieved through grades and standardized tests.	<<Propaganda>>	The relationship between the standardized test/grade and the human being is remote.
Resignation	Bureaucracy is too hard to change.	<<Catastrophizing>>	A sustained campaign is required over time.

The idea of a *network learning environment* is a critical means to transition the art of instruction from information as a primary source of design to interactivity as a primary source of design. The word *network* is an invitation to the strategic planning and coordination of relationships and connections.

A learning environment is *networked* in the sense that the learner is provided with tools, opportunities and possibilities to orchestrate relationships and connections with people, places and things. This provision of tools, opportunities, and possibilities is central to the art of instructional design. The information that ebbs and flows in a network learning environment is a direct result of the quality of interaction taking place. In other words, information is no longer a cause, it is an effect.

The new art of curriculum and instruction originates in interaction design.

The instructional designer of network learning environments has a unified orientation to structure and control in learning. They are mentors of cascading networks of learning and no longer solitary experts of information. The classroom is no longer self-contained but is designed to be a central communications hub that is supported by a broad range of external relationships and connections. The instructional designer leverages network learning environments to support the needs and interests of the learner within the guiding framework of the curriculum. Information is not imposed, it is the network itself.

Interaction Design

Using the web to watch for and assess the developing patterns of change generated by this kind of interaction will, I think, become a prime social requirement in the near future. . . . the way for us to better manage change is to become acquainted with the interactive process. (Burke, James 1996)

What are the building blocks of the interactive process? We must first acknowledge that all information on the Internet is merely a collection of transient digital fodder. There is no need, nor is there any real advantage, to accelerate our lives to the pace of information lifecycles. If this is an acceptable idea, a strategy for developing concrete and practical approaches to interactivity in learning is required. The result of this strategy is a planning framework for the design of network learning environments. Finally, we must ensure that the ideas of *interactivity* and *networks* are not understood as being exclusively associated with technology and the Internet.

Interactivity can be represented and modeled in a wide variety of ways. The *Interaction Design Matrix* presented below provides a framework for thinking about network learning environments from a strategic planning perspective. It looks unfamiliar in the sense that the traditional subject discipline categories, courses, and timetables are absent:

INTERACTION DESIGN MATRIX

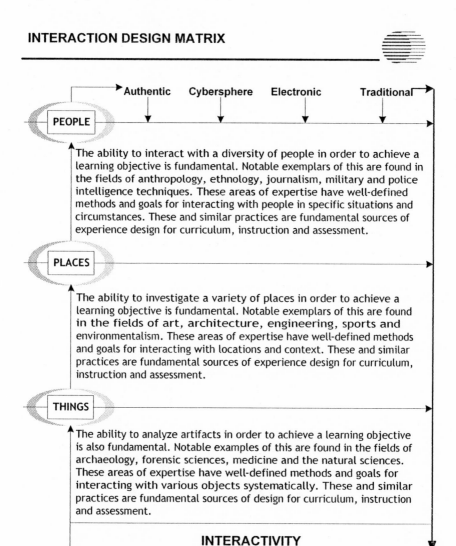

	Authentic	Cybersphere	Electronic	Traditional

PEOPLE

The ability to interact with a diversity of people in order to achieve a learning objective is fundamental. Notable exemplars of this are found in the fields of anthropology, ethnology, journalism, military and police intelligence techniques. These areas of expertise have well-defined methods and goals for interacting with people in specific situations and circumstances. These and similar practices are fundamental sources of experience design for curriculum, instruction and assessment.

PLACES

The ability to investigate a variety of places in order to achieve a learning objective is fundamental. Notable exemplars of this are found in the fields of art, architecture, engineering, sports and environmentalism. These areas of expertise have well-defined methods and goals for interacting with locations and context. These and similar practices are fundamental sources of experience design for curriculum, instruction and assessment.

THINGS

The ability to analyze artifacts in order to achieve a learning objective is also fundamental. Notable examples of this are found in the fields of archaeology, forensic sciences, medicine and the natural sciences. These areas of expertise have well-defined methods and goals for interacting with various objects systematically. These and similar practices are fundamental sources of design for curriculum, instruction and assessment.

INTERACTIVITY

Interaction design is primarily focused on providing a support system for the creation of *primary resource materials*. A primary resource is a body of information that is created by a learner through authentic experience. In network learning environments, the learner is *always* a co-creator of valued information resources.

Four Types of Learning Environments

There are many kinds of environments for learning. Four examples of this are: a) authentic learning environments; b) cybersphere learning environments; c) electronic learning environments; and d) print learning environments. Of course, there are many ways to add, subtract, categorize, and re-categorize these rather artificial boundaries. For example, we could be investigating an environmental situation while at the same time using a wireless device to connect to the Internet making use of books on-site to help interpret the experience.

Authentic Learning Environments
The collection of physical, geographic places and locations that are designed into the learning experience. The idea of on-site investigative research and field work characterize authentic learning. The learner is actually there in the right physical location at the right time.

Cybersphere Learning Environments
The collection of digitally networked environments for communications, collaboration and information access. The Internet is the technological foundation of the Cybersphere. The learner is virtually there and has an interactive proximity to the people, places, and things involved in an event or activity.

Electronic Learning Environments
The collection of electronic environments outside of the realm of the Internet. The learner is still to a degree virtually there, but more often in terms of viewing the content created by someone else.

Print Learning Environments
The collection of alphabetic environments that are disseminated through print technologies and distribution mechanisms.

In a traditional instructional design paradigm, the horizontal access would contain subject disciplines and sub-topics rather than environments. In this sense, the architecture of the learning environment is a replacement for the architecture of information.

People, Places and Things

This sequence of people, places, and things provides a framework for instructional design in network learning environments. As mentioned in the Interaction Design Matrix, there are many excellent real-life models, methods, and processes that can be invited through people, places, and things. Of course, we never solely experience people, places, and things independently from each other.

People
The people we seek to interact with are the first and most important source of interactivity in learning. A network learning environment is first and foremost focused on the facilitating relationships across a diversity of people. The critical skill sets for the learner are all those that help them to create, interact, and develop primary information resources through their interaction with people.

Places
The places we seek to learn in are the second most important source of interactivity in learning environments. The learner is a nomad; an individual that is expert in traveling physically and technologically in order to pursue a motivation for learning. This aspect of interactivity represents a significant challenge for the organizational design and administration of learning.

Things
The things (i.e. objects and artifacts) we seek to learn with are the third most important source of interactivity in learning environments. The things collected by the learner provide another means to develop primary information resources through observation, analysis, inference, and deduction. This approach is more akin to the investigative strategies of the police detective or the archaeologist.

The traditional instructional design paradigm would refer to *knowledge*, *skills*, and *attitudes* instead of *people*, *places*, and *things*. In this sense, interaction design is a replacement for the traditional aims commonly found in education and training.

Emergence

All networks have emergent properties, or events and actions that we begin to see only as they occur. A network learning environment has a number of emergent properties that provide the basis for a sustainable campaign to transition our design sensibilities away from information to interactivity.

One of the first things to emerge through the idea of interaction design is conflict with well-entrenched practices and traditions of education and training. This is in no way surprising since interaction design is designed to probe and therefore create a sense of conflict with current practices in instructional design and delivery. For example, a criticism of interaction design as a replacement for information design might be that it is untested and theoretical. An answer to this question would include the fact that there is little else in our world more untested and theoretical than information. We might criticize the rather dramatic implication for change implied in relation to the heavy investments of time and money already given to the information-based paradigm. An answer to this would point out that leaders and decision-makers that allow themselves to be mired in bureaucratic and political objectives at the expense of real growth and improvement are not leaders. And the cycle of point–counterpoint would continue. . . .

More importantly, what really begins to emerge from the idea of network learning environments are fundamentally new opportunities and possibilities for learning. These opportunities and possibilities are not merely the "variation on a theme" type but a complete recalibration and freeing of our minds by "going back to zero" in terms of our thinking about the art and science of instructional design. In the end, what we are really attempting to accomplish is the creation of a new narrative for the stories of learning, education, and training. The idea of a *network learning environment* is really a new kind of cultural identity. The idea of interaction design naturally invites critical and creative vitality.

The network learning environment, then, is the nucleus of the art of instructional design. The source of energy for instruction is interaction design. The result is a new set of situations and circumstances for learning itself:

EMERGENT PROPERTIES OF NETWORK LEARNING ENVIRONMENTS

Curriculum

The system of curriculum development outlined in *Part One: Learning* originates in narrative, critical and creative vitality. The "what" or "content" of learning originates in exemplary narratives that serve as a source of inspiration and action in modern life. Curriculum originates in the lives of people, not in information.

Instruction

Instructional design is focused on the creation of interactivity not the delivery of knowledge, skills and attitudes associated with subject disciplines. The traditional teacher-student relationship is abandoned; all participants in a network learning environment are called *learners* and are therefore simultaneously both teachers and students. The power, control and structure of a networked learning environment is the distributed responsibility of all participants.

Organization

The organizational design required to support these new principles of curriculum and instruction is a network in itself; bureaucratic structures are abandoned for network operational structures for all participants. Any institution involved in learning is a communications hub and a center for innovation.

Evaluation

The idea of assessing and measuring students against standardized information-based criteria is abandoned for an approach that establishes performance criteria for interactivity in learning. The idea of performance is centered on the creation of network learning environments; evaluation and professional development are pervasive and inseparable activities of any network learning environment.

How do we navigate ourselves through these emerging properties that ebb and flow throughout a network learning environment? How do people really need to be prepared to be successful in this interactive and dynamic landscape? *Chapter 5: The Network Explorers* develops a strategy for ensuring success.

Strategic Directions: Network Learning Environments

ELIMINATE PLANNING METHODS CENTERED ON INFORMATION

There is no proven basis that information typologies and the resulting series of subject disciplines and expertise is the best means to design and organize learning.

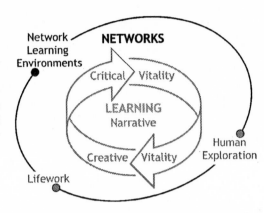

INTERACTIVITY IS THE NEW SOURCE OF DESIGN FOR CURRICULUM AND INSTRUCTION

Interactivity is the primary source of design for network learning environments. The focus for all learners regardless of their age and ability is to develop the skill of interaction design in order to create primary information resources. Secondary information resources are integrated into learning as they are required.

DESIGN AND IMPLEMENTATION ARE A DISTRIBUTED RESPONSIBILITY

Education and training systems cannot continue to operate in isolation. Corporations can no longer merely sponsor education as a means to extend their brands. Government can no longer treat education as an isolated area of policy development. Cultural institutions can no longer merely provide places of observation for education. Cross-functional alliances and learning networks must be established to share intelligence in order to create the foundation for a new paradigm in learning.

UNIFIED NETWORKS OF LEARNING

All education systems are inexorably bound by the fact that they provide education to large numbers of people. The idea of a school or school district becomes increasingly irrelevant through networks. Each school and school district is a creator of e-Learning networks, they are not merely participants in e-Learning networks provided by the government or corporations. This means that the idea of a school becomes equated with a global communications hub, a cultural center for innovation, a tactical response unit to social issues, and an active and visible community force. Unified networks of learning can only occur if they are completely aware and in attendance of the present moment in the world.

COLLECT AND DISSEMINATE EXEMPLARY NARRATIVES OF NETWORK LEARNING

The provision of narratives that capture and elevate the human-built networks and how they are technologically supported in order to address the needs specific people in specific circumstances is a replacement for abstract generalizations about social action.

5. THE NETWORK EXPLORERS

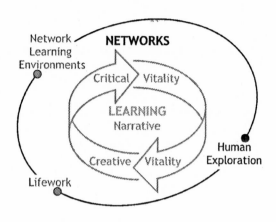

All learners are explorers; we do not learn unless we explore. To observe a person learning is to view the ways in which they are exploring their present circumstances. The most fundamental and important aim of any instructional design methodology is to promote the improvement of abilities such as investigating, discovering and inventing. Improving the learner's capacity for *exploration* is the single most important reference point for instructional design. The primary objective of the instructional designer is to establish life-long and lifewide structures for the development of human ingenuity.

What are the most essential and fundamental abilities for learners to develop in order to fully leverage network learning environments?

Our world is rich in narratives of people making discoveries and embarking on quests and journeys. These are not merely stories to be read, but more importantly comprise a fundamental repertoire of real-life methods, models, processes, and tools for exploration in authentic situations and circumstances. If we were to build a generic set of "skills" that were aimed at being universal, nothing less than human ingenuity would provide a strong enough foundation.

Chapter Design

Learning Scenarios
A scenario sets the stage for learning by defining specific situations and circumstances for exploration. The issues originate in modern life and the exploration itself is literally placed under surveillance.

Human Ingenuity

Our inventive skills, cleverness, and imagination facilitate insight into our sur-rounding conditions, the recognition of possibilities, the apprehension of vari-ables, and the capacity for taking action. Without ingenuity, we are held hostage to a reactive lifestyle.

Performance

Real-life examples of exploration in modern life are the living processes where we practice the fundamental methods, processes, and skills for learning. We do not require more textbooks and lectures; we do require more authentic experi-ences and living examples.

For a (person) to attain an eminent degree in learning costs him time, watching, hunger, nakedness, dizziness in the head, weakness in the stomach, and other inconveniences. (Cervantes, Miguel de 1993)

Exploration is the most meaningful response to the confluence of modern life. When we face the reality of the events that take place in our lives we become explorers constantly striving *to attain an eminent degree in learning*. If we choose not to stand and face the reality of the events that take place in our lives, we become cave dwellers. To explore means to find the courage, assume the risk, desire to understand, search for meaning, discover a solu-tion, to take action for and against, and most of all to feel alive. A person engaged in an exploration is the most concrete observable sign of the phe-nomenon of learning.

At its summit, all explorers are intimately tied to a guiding narrative. For example, Erik Weihenmayer's conquest of Mount Everest is symbolic of a lifelong heroic journey through the reality of his own circumstances in life. His degree in learning clearly cost a variety of inconveniences, but his desire to literally and symbolically explore the confluence of his life is easily observ-able. The same may be said of Stephen Biko, yet more than confronting inconveniences, he had his life taken from him. Erik Weihenmayer and Stephen Biko are two different people from two different cultures facing completely different circumstances driven by their own individual goals and aspirations. At the same time, there is a great deal more in common between these two people than there are differences. This unity and sense of connect-edness originates in the exploration of life itself.

5. The Network Explorers

Many educational and training programs teach methods such as problem-solving, conflict resolution, decision-making, life skills, time management, organizational skills, leadership skills, collaborative group skills, stress management, thinking skills, and a range of others. Very often, these abilities are delivered to students without ever having them leave the building, and often without ever having them leave their chairs. Very often, the intended benefit is to intellectually equip people in these various capacities. Very often, these abilities are taught without ever referring to how real people have used them in real situations, leading us to wonder if they really exist at all. These activities are definitely a kind of exploration, yet the exploration is completely distanced from their living context. Where are the challenges, opportunities, journeys, discoveries, successes, and failures of real people in all of this? Where are the guiding narratives we need to hold on to in the confluence of modern life? Are we making the assumption that by equipping people with these abstract cognitive tools we are in some manner effectively preparing them for the world they will face?

To be fully engaged in an exploration is to be fully engaged in a narrative of discovery. The educational reductionist would have us believe that by reducing ideas and processes to their most elemental units that we arrive at something that has value on its own. There is little value in anything that is presented outside of its actual context. The fundamental direction of Exploration, and therefore learning itself, is the ongoing synthesis of connections, relationships, associations, and variables across our experiences. Exploration, with respect to learning, can be nothing less than this.

The three styles of exploration below are a mere glimpse of the breadth and depth of possibilities. What is more important here is to make a close connection between a style of exploration and its authentic reality. The reason for this is to create a foundation that avoids the presentation of abstract methods, skills, and competencies in the absence of their authentic context. More simply, we learn to explore by immersing ourselves as best we can in genuine exploration. The opposite is also true. We do *not* learn to explore by following generic models of exploratory processes (e.g. problem-solving models, decision-making models, conflict resolution models, etc.) that are removed from their authentic context. Generic models lead to armchair abstraction; field work, simulations, and case studies bring us closer to authenticity. It is obvious to say that we cannot provide authentic experiences in many situations. At the same time, it is clearly not enough to merely follow abstract processes in a textbook.

A VIGNETTE OF HUMAN EXPLORATION

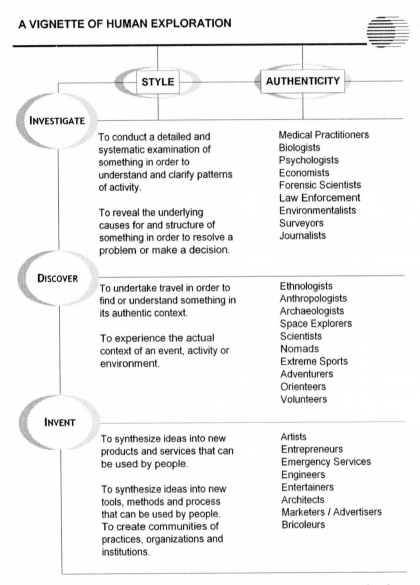

	STYLE	AUTHENTICITY
INVESTIGATE	To conduct a detailed and systematic examination of something in order to understand and clarify patterns of activity. To reveal the underlying causes for and structure of something in order to resolve a problem or make a decision.	Medical Practitioners Biologists Psychologists Economists Forensic Scientists Law Enforcement Environmentalists Surveyors Journalists
DISCOVER	To undertake travel in order to find or understand something in its authentic context. To experience the actual context of an event, activity or environment.	Ethnologists Anthropologists Archaeologists Space Explorers Scientists Nomads Extreme Sports Adventurers Orienteers Volunteers
INVENT	To synthesize ideas into new products and services that can be used by people. To synthesize ideas into new tools, methods and process that can be used by people. To create communities of practices, organizations and institutions.	Artists Entrepreneurs Emergency Services Engineers Entertainers Architects Marketers / Advertisers Bricoleurs

It is the power of narrative that provides the necessary unity and coherence for exploration. An exploration is fundamentally a story about the challenges and opportunities in someone's life. If we connect ourselves to a repertoire of real stories about real explorations then we increase the potential for elevating the quality of our own lives.

5. The Network Explorers

Shining the Light

A *theatre* is a building, room or outdoor structure that is used for the presentation of stories. A script forms the basis for the production and to exercise control over the performance itself. Without a script the performance would be improvised. The script is a kind of intermediary between the writer and performers. The challenge for the performers is to bring the words in the script back to life. This is similar to a musician interpreting the printed musical score of a composer. The stage is designed and controlled to portray the essence of various scenes and settings. Audiences are spectators that create their own meaning about the performance through the overall effect of the scenario created.

A scenario is not scripted in literal terms and requires the improvisatory spirit to energize it. Modern life scenarios are built from a collage of explicit and tacit cultural beliefs that present an environment for living. The cultural script is similar to a jazz fake book that provides an outline of the melody and chord progression, but the actual performance is left to the individual. The *cultural fake book* consists of policies, laws, citizenship, religions, customs, traditions, expectations, norms, rules, health, education, entertainment, employment, and technology. People ebb and flow through a variety of places such as home, family, church, the workplace, movie theatres, parks, shopping malls, and in some cases regions, nations, and the world itself.

The phenomenon of learning is more closely related to improvisation than it is to the interpretation of a written script. The emergent properties of modern life are *the stories of our lives*. These are the stories we use to explain ourselves to ourselves and to provide guidance through the collage of situations and circumstances presented to us in life. Many musicians who improvise think of their art as a kind of storytelling. The news media, government policies, corporate business plans, and religion are all kinds of narratives designed to explain ourselves to ourselves. Knowledge is not power unless it has a story to tell.

There is a human tendency to fall prey to the hallucination that the more life is scripted and "structured" the more control we have over it. The desire for control over our circumstances is a primordial survival instinct. It is obviously important for any society to have rules and protocols in order to be functional; however, we should never assume that what is scripted is the same thing as what actually happens: "So let it be written, and then we'll hope it gets done." Education is clearly over-scripted. If we place the prescriptions for education in the face of the unscripted and improvisatory nature of life outside of schooling, we see a dramatic difference in the context, situation, and circumstances of learning. The controlled processes of schooling have little resemblance to the fluid processes of life outside of school. This is one reason why students experience a culture shock upon leaving school. The key to preparation for society is to more closely integrate schooling with that society. If modern life is dynamic, variable, and improvisatory in nature, then the ways in which we structure learning, education, and training should possess the same qualities.

> **Light is going to shine into nearly every corner of our lives. (Brin, David 1998)**

The technological and cultural impact of *surveillance* is fundamental to the design of learning scenarios. We are already immersed in various kinds of surveillance, or situations in which we have a sense of being *watched or observed* for some purpose. The wireless camera, the autonomous robot, the satellite, Internet transactions, and news programs are the network symbols of surveillance today. These technologies are extensions of our eyes, ears, and bodies and are designed to help us watch and potentially interact with something from a strategically remote (or safe) location. We gain new insights into the activities of people as well as develop an increased sensitivity about the ways we ourselves are being watched.

The possible ways that people, places, and things can be put under surveillance is dramatic. It is not enough to read or view diagrams about surveillance—one must explore the experience of it. For example, to learn about the relationship of remote cameras to surveillance, the learner must be able to function both as the one being observed and the one doing the observing. One obvious perspective on this is to understand how surveillance operates as a technological system. It can also be considered from a social and psychological perspective. An exploration would then consist of authentic experiences using a remote-controlled camera system that allows the learner to do the watching and to be watched. For example, a close connection now exists between the increased levels of school violence and the integration of surveillance systems to reduce violent events. The school environment as a whole can be thought of as an opportunity to design a learning environment for exploring surveillance in which the idea of watching others and being watched is equally distributed across everyone (administrators, security personnel, teachers, students, parents).

The technological reality of surveillance is of far less interest than the social and emotional issues that arise between privacy and accountability—"Whenever a conflict arises between privacy and accountability, people demand the former for themselves and the latter for everybody else." (Brin, David 1998) It is important that we understand the ways in which we are being *watched* if only to be better aware, but it is more important to understand the ways in which we ourselves can watch others. This has nothing to do with fearful attitudes of *self-protection*, but has everything to do with the development of the powers of exploration. In fact, any *fear* we might have in relation to the idea of surveillance needs to be rationalized. It is not helpful for people to *have the feeling of being watched* in a way that invokes an internal sense of fear and mistrust.

> *Attention! Here and now! That's what you always forget, isn't it? You forget to pay attention to what's happening. And that's the same as not being here and now. (Huxley, Aldous 1962)*

While network technologies help us extend our powers of observation in new ways, the idea of surveillance is of course not limited to the high-tech industry. The ways in which our learning has traditionally been watched is largely through the surveillance of assessment and evaluation. The IQ test is an entirely useless form of surveillance designed to reduce people's minds to numbers. Standardized testing is a tactic used in education systems to place people under surveillance. The result is that private and public identity becomes a series of entries in a data base. The report card is a symbol of making our private selves public to our family members, school personnel, prospective employers, and the government. One of the most fundamental problems with this approach to evaluation is that those responsible for creating and administering these standardized tests are not placed under the same kind of surveillance. They remain in the shadows and are not transparent in the process. Our entire experience of being educated or trained is branded by standardization. It is quite apparent that assessment and evaluation are a means to place people who are suspected of being engaged in learning under surveillance in order to ensure they conform to the imposed standard.

Attendance is another common object of surveillance. In school, our attendance is tracked and recorded. The result is a record of our physical presence in a school over a number of years. In business, the notion of taking attendance is almost as prominent, and the idea of surveillance is technologically more sophisticated. Every action on a computer, every phone call, every fax, every financial transaction, every training course provides an electronic footprint that can be used to track our workplace activities. The beneficial viewpoint on assessment is that knowledge of a person's attendance patterns is useful information in diagnosing and providing students and workers with feedback to help them improve. The negative viewpoint on assessment is that it can be used as a means to control and imprison people.

Throughout our schooling, our attendance is reported to our parents on a report card. If there is a more immediate problem, it is reported via the telephone. Since school attendance is expected, a lack of attendance is commonly indicated as a problem. The issue of absence becomes even more prominent in a high school setting where it is easier for students to select those courses or teachers they wish to attend, and those they don't. Beyond our schooling, we are expected to attend a normal workday of eight hours or more. Perhaps it is not until we reach retirement that the expectations on attendance in our lives are finally relaxed and we can attend to life itself. By this time, our attendance in life is in closer proximity to the universal standardized test of our own end.

Physical absence is a guarantee that we are not paying attention. We can also be absent in mind. In other words, we can be physically present and meet the requirement for attendance, but mentally absent and fail to meet the requirements for attention. The rebuke "Pay Attention!" captures this idea of physical presence and intellectual absence. Physical absence (excepting reasons of illness or other extenuating circumstances) is an advertisement of opposition to something; it is a public declaration that the individual perceives the experience as irrelevant or unimportant. Intellectual absence is different in kind only; it is a private statement of opposition. If we are thinking of things other than what we are directed to, we are nevertheless engaged in a genuine learning process. Being physically or intellectually absent is not necessarily a sign of negativity or passivity; it may sometimes be a very normal, healthy, and necessary reaction to the imposition of external demands that have no relevance. It may, at a more primordial level, be an echo of the *fight or flight* instinct itself.

The quality of participation is another common object of surveillance in education and the workplace. Attendance merely determines whether or not we are physically present—"Is the person here?" Participation is a means to look at the quality of the effort we put into our work when we are physically present—"Is the person performing to the best of their ability?" A common metric used to determine the quality of a person's participation is on-task versus off-task behavior. The criteria for making judgments about the quality of participation are typically referenced against the aims and goals of a curriculum or job description. On-task characteristics include things that relate to positive contributions to the stated goals. Off-task characteristics and behaviors are generally seen as not being in support of the stated goals. What is important to keep in mind is that on-task behaviors can be motivated by high levels of interest and relevance as much as they are by high levels conformity and submission. Off-task behaviors can in fact be an indicator of a highly motivated and capable individual.

An artifact of education and training refers to the things produced or activities undertaken (i.e. examinations, tests, worksheets, assignments, presentation materials, essays, artwork, notes taken in a notebook, message board contributions, chat records, email history, video-conferencing recordings—anything that is designed to capture a performance) by students and workers. Assessing and evaluating the artifacts of learning is considered to be the meeting place between the intended goals of the curriculum to the actual performance of the students. In other words, it is a means of competitively comparing performance. It is also a means to assess and evaluate the individual teacher, program of study, school, school district, trainer, training program, and courseware.

When we know we are being watched, we become more vigilant with our attention. We know that those watching us are representative of a set of requirements or demands on us. If we choose or are forced to conform to these requirements, our presence of mind can be supportive, neutral, or in opposition. For example, creative teachers may not wish to have their teaching conform to the requirements of standardized examinations; however, they may adjust their thinking and behavior to support the exam as they know their own success is connected to it. This is called on the one hand ensuring career success, and on the other career survival. It is not different in kind for students.

Human Ingenuity

If a learner is to improve his ability to learn, he is fundamentally engaged in a process that is designed to improve and enhance his own ingenuity in responding to the confluence of modern life. A person that is *ingenious* is considered to be clever, shrewd, talented, imaginative, capable, and inventive in both thought *and* action. None of these qualities have any correlation in our technologies. An ingenious person lives for the present moment. They pay attention to the situations in which they find themselves. They attend to the circumstances they face. They have the courage and assume the risk of being fully present in the events taking place in their own lives. Human ingenuity constantly seeks to shine the brightest light possible on the world.

The sad reality is that the styles of instructional design found in our systems of education and training have little to do with the promotion of human ingenuity. This is in no way surprising given the fact that these systems do not originate in the experiences of people, but in the experience of information. There is little value in exploring information in an abstract context. Compounding this problem is the inability of these systems to function in a proactive and adaptive manner in direct response to what is happening in the world at that moment. Information-based systems of learning unavoidably force all participants into a highly reactive and repetitive mode, a mode which does not support the development of ingenuity in people.

> *Attention! Here and now! That's what you always forget, isn't it? You forget to pay attention to what's happening. And that's the same as not being here and now. (Huxley, Aldous 1962)*

None of this is to say that the learners confined to information bureaucracies (i.e. students, teachers, administrators, curriculum and instructional designers, and decision-makers) are not ingenious. It is to say, however, that their ingenuity is largely confined to situations and circumstances outside the confines of the system in which they find themselves. The primacy of information in our systems of education and training continue to churn away largely in complete ignorance of the events taking place in our world. This creates a false sense of structure and security. There are many events that take place in the world which lead us to the point of no return. In moments like this we pass the crossroad between what was and what now must be. A profound example of this is the pathetic act of terrorism launched in the United States on September 11, 2001. It is completely impossible to avoid both the horror and power of the human spirit in this circumstance. Yet at the same time, the information-based curriculum that shapes our education and training systems finds itself completely stymied and confused by the real world. We struggle to react to the confluence in our world and steadfastly maintain the same diet of language, math, science, history, and the like. We struggle to implement educational "emergency response" mechanisms to help limit the psychological damage the world can cause to people. We believe these subject disciplines to be safe, but they are not. We believe these subject disciplines to be fundamental preparation, but they are not. We believe these subject disciplines to provide a stable and durable foundation for learning, but they do not.

We all need to return to *ground zero*. If each of us were to physically stand in face of the reality of September 11, 2001 we could only conclude that world as a unified entity is not sane. This, however, is a far better and more hopeful conclusion than allowing the stable diet of the information machine to provide a means to escape this conclusion. Of course and most importantly, there are serious implications of these events for the psychological well being of people. We are all forced to stand in a very direct line of sight with fear itself. We are also forced to stand in a very direct line with hope as well. When history is so obviously and fundamentally altered forever, so should our systems of learning.

The most fundamental problem we face is simple to articulate, and easy to develop a value proposition for, but challenging to implement. The problem is this: our systems of learning are almost completely aimed at abstractions about past events and information about the world. The solution is to aim our systems of learning on real events of the present moment and the kinds of meaning and understanding people can create. Information abstractions only have value if they offer insight into the present moment. Past events of humankind only have value if they serve to clarify and help construct meaning about the present moment. The present moment is not only defined by the horrific, but also by the wondrous. Just as we should not hide behind information in tragic times, we should also not hide behind information in times of celebration.

Human ingenuity, then, is the primary source of instructional design. The systems, methods, structures, organizations, processes, and tools we use to support learning must be completely unified by this prime directive. The network learning environment, in contrast to the traditional classroom environment, is the most effective way to create the basic context for this kind of instruction. The learner, as an explorer, stands in full view of the present moment, leverages knowledge about the past to clarify meaning and understanding, and develops strategic action plans for affecting the future in a positive way. The timeline for learning is present-past-future not past-present-future.

How do we plan for the promotion of human ingenuity as learning? What is the most effective organizational design to support human ingenuity? How do we assess the value of an instructional design process that originates in human ingenuity?

The means to answer these questions brings us back full circle to the question of learning itself. In *Part One: Learning* I characterized the phenomenon of learning as a quest for narrative that is engaged through the critical and creative vitality of people. The rationale for this is that narrative is the most important means available to us for building meaningful connections and relationships to our private and public identities. Identity is itself a network of stories. I opened *Part Two: Networks* with the idea of the *Network Learning Environment*. This is an organizational design framework to support learning. When we invite people into this system of thought, the development of ingenuity becomes the primary activity and daily focus for instructional delivery. In other words, ingenuity, not information is the content for learning.

The idea of educating people through the improvement of their *knowledge, skills,* and *attitudes* symbolizes the traditional approach to curriculum and instructional design. The paradigm is essentially one that: a) teaches predefined areas of knowledge that are thought to be required by the general population; b) teaches students the skills to comprehend and communicate the core areas of knowledge; c) teaches attitudes to support the individual and collaborative development of knowledge and skill; and d) uses standardized forms of assessment to determine how successful the student was in relation to the above requirements. This model is one that exists almost independently of the most current and relevant events taking place in the world. In other words, current events are acknowledged to some degree, but the inflexible and unresponsive structure of curriculum and instructional design churn away regardless. The most obvious indicator proving this point to be true is the timetable for learning; the ways in which education and training systems divide time into mechanical components continues to remain dominant regardless of the events taking place around us. The opportunity for being creative with the use of time in response to the world is nearly nonexistent in this paradigm.

As a direct result of this, the development of human ingenuity is forced to occur outside of the imposed timetable. A timetable that is not dynamic, flexible, adaptive, and responsive to the events taking place in the world confines people to an information assembly line. Structures of knowledge that do not originate in the events taking place around us confine people to wither in the past, to the abstraction of experience, or both. Skill sets designed only to support and promote imposed structures of knowledge further entrench isolation from the real world. Attitudes designed to make people feel good and positive about this kind of experience are a form of manipulation.

The most important strategy for bringing human ingenuity to the center stage of learning is to develop support mechanisms for a greater range of interactivity throughout the curriculum and instructional design process. Simply stated, the *knowledge-skills-attitudes paradigm* should be replaced with a *people-places-things paradigm* as described in the interaction design matrix above. In other words, the design, planning, implementation, and assessment cycle for learning no longer originates in the traditional information paradigm, and it is here that we now stand on ground zero.

Human ingenuity is a real-time event, therefore the source of design for learning, education, and training originate in the real-time events taking place in our world. It is structured on a foundation of interactivity across people, places, and things. Information is not a real-time event. The propaganda of "information anytime, anywhere" or "just the right information in just the right amount at just the right time" is merely an extension of the industrial-age paradigm of education and training. It is structured on the uniform distribution of knowledge, skills, and attitudes. The ways in which people perform in network learning environments focused on the development of human ingenuity versus the ways in which people perform in bureaucratic learning environments focused on the dissemination of information are fundamentally different.

THE HUMAN INGENUITY PARADIGM

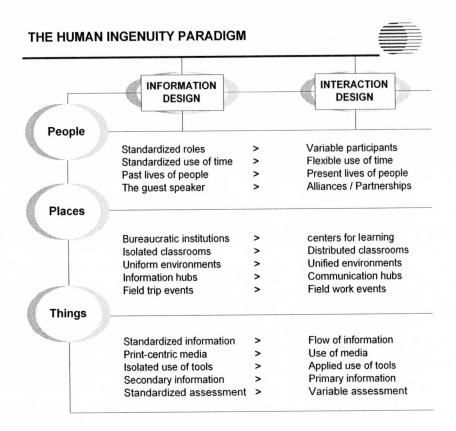

	INFORMATION DESIGN		INTERACTION DESIGN
People			
	Standardized roles	>	Variable participants
	Standardized use of time	>	Flexible use of time
	Past lives of people	>	Present lives of people
	The guest speaker	>	Alliances / Partnerships
Places			
	Bureaucratic institutions	>	centers for learning
	Isolated classrooms	>	Distributed classrooms
	Uniform environments	>	Unified environments
	Information hubs	>	Communication hubs
	Field trip events	>	Field work events
Things			
	Standardized information	>	Flow of information
	Print-centric media	>	Use of media
	Isolated use of tools	>	Applied use of tools
	Secondary information	>	Primary information
	Standardized assessment	>	Variable assessment

Performance

What are the concrete and practical reference points for human ingenuity? The answer is to look out into the world and see what is going on. While making the final revisions on this book, I was constantly peering out into the world of terrorism through the media. The tragic events of September 11, 2001 in the United States have caused a permanent change in our world, the specifics of which will emerge over a long period of time. The deaths caused in this event have caused a collective sense of bereavement. At the same time, the strength and courage of many international leaders, emergency services personnel, and the families and friends of the victims is incredible. When we observe the wide range of people dedicating themselves to being a part of the solution in these extremely dark times we see a celebration of the marvel of human ingenuity. There are completely new and unique networks of relationships taking place in our world. There are new lines of communications being forged. There are new systems of support for the well being of people emerging. Organizations and institutions are being synthesized in order to develop intelligence more effectively. Our belief systems and shared values are being restructured. The economy is rapidly trying to adapt and stabilize. We become more familiar with journalists and reporters in the far reaches of the world. We are all witnessing the emergence of a system of exploration that seems to have no historical precedent.

It will be interesting to see if our education system changes in any fundamental way, even though the world it exists in has already changed forever. Of course, protecting people from the deep levels of stress and trauma caused by this event is something that requires a great deal of care. At the same time, having the curriculum and instructional process churn away with only minor breaks for care-giving is a recipe for disaster. In speaking to students in high schools I have found no discernible change in the operations of the school as a result of September 11, 2001. We might think this constitutes an attempt to "keep our lives as normal as possible." It is in no way normal to maintain a curriculum that does not adapt to and integrate the events that have taken place. In fact, this is completely abnormal and unhealthy.

While these tragic acts of terrorism are now pervasive in our collective experience and must result in curriculum change and growth, the idea of human ingenuity need not originate in the tragic and horrible. We can easily seek other models that are "safer" in character. If we again look out into the world and ask the question, "Who are the people and what are the roles that provide examples for human ingenuity?" we can identify various categories of performance:

⇒ **The Ethnologist**
The comparative investigation of cultures including the use of language, religious orientations, social patterns, artistic expression, and use of technology.

⇒ **The Archaeologist**
The systemic recovery and analysis of cultural artifacts through the use of technology.

⇒ **The Journalist**
The creation and dissemination of primary information resources about current news and information through on-site research and interviews.

⇒ **The Criminal Investigator**
The use of deductive and inductive reasoning in order to understand the motives, causes, and effects of human actions and behaviors.

⇒ **The Artist**
The creation and communication of unusual insights and perceptions about the human condition.

⇒ **The Human Rights Activist**
The use of human networks in order to relieve and eliminate atrocities in various parts of the world.

⇒ **The Psychologist**
The diagnosis, treatment, and prevention of physical and psychological illness.

⇒ **The Politician**
The structure, methods, and effectiveness of decision-making for large groups of people.

⇒ **The Entrepreneur**
The structure, methods, and effectiveness of profit-generation for individuals and organizations.

⇒ **The Entertainer**
The ways, means, and effects of producing media designed for commercial entertainment.

This list is only a glimpse of the possibilities. It is important to note that I have referred to the role being performed rather than the subject category. For example, it is more important to refer to the *journalist* than the subject *journalism*. The first is a direct reference to the specific experiences of a real person, the second is a direct reference to the abstract concepts that define the area of study. A person is capable of performance, a subject discipline is not. This naturally leads to the identification of real people that serve as exemplars and provide the most important "content" for learning. For example, a stellar individual like CNN's Christiane Amanpour would clearly provide an exceptional foundation for learning about the journalist as a narrative, not journalism as information. This difference between these two seemingly slight shifts in perspective is quite profound.

Living models of human ingenuity are not merely abstract generalizations of imaginary processes, but are intimately connected to specific kinds of situations and circumstances. It is not the model of the process that is of importance, it is the real experience of people actively conducting these processes that is of critical value. It is obvious to say that mastering an abstract model of a process in no way means that the individual has mastered the dynamics of the process to which the model points.

The real *teachers* in our world are the people that provide authentic examples of human ingenuity. This is a dramatically different orientation from the notion of a teacher who is a subject discipline expert and who may have extensive information and knowledge about a particular field, but may not have authentic depth of involvement in it. As an explorer, the teacher can no longer be a passive and literate observer of other people's activities in order to translate that to a student audience; the teacher of the future is an individual who is quite literally immersed in participation. Without this immersion, the teacher will always be forced to represent an unnecessary layer of intermediation between their students and the events taking place in the world itself.

This perspective on what it means to be a *teacher* is fundamental to elevating the status of the profession. Current practices in teacher preparation and professional development encourage, unfortunately, the view of a teacher as an observer and an intermediary. There is absolutely no basis for a statement such as, "Those that can, do. Those that can't, teach." This quip says nothing about the profession of teaching itself, but says everything about inadequate and immature cultural attitudes toward education and training. We should say, "Those that can, do. Those that can't do will learn to do." Equally problematic is the notion that teachers can somehow be replaced by technologies. It would be fair to say that the role and areas of focus for a teacher definitely evolve through technological innovation, but the idea of replacing and reducing the population of teachers is entirely ignorant. The fact that our systems of teacher preparation and professional development are wholly inadequate to this task is not a reflection on the person that is a teacher, but is simply a statement on the inadequacy and immaturity of our own understanding about what a teacher is.

I look forward to a night on the town, maybe a date even, but more than anything I think about how I will really sleep for the first time in five nights, how I will allow myself to let go of my students—the ones who never turn in any work despite my calls home, the ones who won't sit still and can't stop talking, the ones who work diligently every day and never get any praise they deserve because I am too frantic and disorganized to worry about anyone except those who aren't "meeting the standard." . . . I tried every angle, and slowly I became less understanding and more frustrated and threatening. (Kantrowitz, Barbara 2001)

The result of the teacher sentenced to a life of intermediation is frustration, resentment, and eventually exhaustion and depression. There is no other possible result in a system that places information, subject discipline expertise, mindless routines and schedules, standardized testing, unsupportive and ill-equipped parents, and status quo administrators in positions of power. What happens is that the output of an entire system of disorganization eventually collides with the emotional well being of the teacher and the student. The level of conflict in this battle ground for the human sensibilities is substantial and is not disconnected from instances of violence and hatred. People, in this system, have little if any opportunity to construct their narrative and therefore their own identity since their sense of identity is quite literally imposed upon them.

In his book, *The Transparent Society: Will Technology Force Us to Choose Between Privacy and Freedom?* David Brin compassionately notes that, "It is hard for recent cave dwellers to transform themselves into smart, honest, and truly independent creatures of light." (Brin, David 1998) It is the conflict between what we desire to be private and what becomes increasingly more public. And this conflict is as much emotional as it is political and technological. The surveillance society may be characterized as an age of accountability. Brin's proposed solution to this challenge is captured in the phrase "reciprocal transparency solutions" which simply means that the power of the watcher is reciprocated in the watched; we are all better off simultaneously watching our watching. In other words, surveillance itself is an open and free interchange.

The exhaustion of teachers and the denigration of the teaching profession must be made transparent. The often deep sense of entitlement in the absence of a deep sense of responsibility in the student population must be made transparent. The support and lack of support from parents in raising their children must be made transparent. As a means to extend our powers of observation to the world and capture real-time processes systems of learning, we need to reduce the gap between what we consider to be private and what we consider to be public. As a means to question our own identity, we will need to become more transparent in our thinking and challenge our underlying assumptions and biases in both critical and creative ways. Shining the light into the dark areas of education is a process full of promise. In fact, it is learning that is the source of energy for the light itself.

Strategic Directions: Network Explorers

ELIMINATE THE DOMINANCE OF "KNOWLEDGE-SKILLS-ATTITUDE"

Learning is far more than the acquisition of knowledge, the mastery of skills, and the development of positive attitudes.

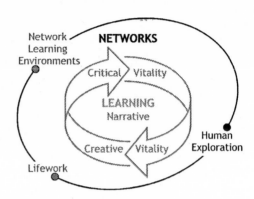

PROMOTE THE IDEA OF INTERACTIVITY

The Interaction Design Matrix makes demands on the ability of people to explore. The idea of the network explorer replaces the idea of the student in the classroom.

DIVERSIFY THE RANGE OF EXPERIENCES IN LEARNING

Traditional approaches are highly print-centric. Experience design demands a diversity of authentic, cybersphere, electronic and print experiences in order to create an effective environment in which learning can occur.

ELIMINATE STANDARDIZED APPROACHES TO ASSESSMENT AND EVALUATION

Standardized tests have nothing to offer; the performance of a person on a test is not an indicator of the performance in actual situations and circumstances. All testing is a collaborative process which is completely integrated with strategic action planning.

COLLECT AND DISSEMINATE EXEMPLARY NARRATIVES OF HUMAN INGENUITY

The provision of narratives that capture and elevate the human ingenuity of specific people in specific circumstances is a replacement for abstract models and generalizations about human intelligence.

6. LIFEWORK

Lifework is the guiding philosophical force for our use of
networks. It is the practical,
concrete and observable representation of our learning as
seen throughout our daily lives.
As an economic strategy, lifework is the single most important means to design and construct a systemic support
system for employability skills
and career directions.

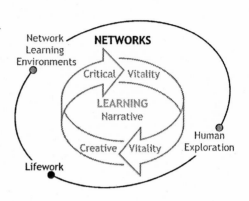

*What is the underlying ground for living a creative and fulfill-
ing life?*

The idea of employability is reduced to the mere acquisition of isolated and
transient skills sets, or competencies. The idea of a career is often a reactive
response to existing opportunities in the workforce. Lifework is a fundamental point of reference for making decisions about employment and career
management.

Chapter Design

Employability
If a person is to be considered employable, they need to possess more than
mere skill sets. Highly intelligent people are often on the periphery of society in
the sense that they do not necessarily accept the established norm and status
quo.

Career Sensibility
Ultimately, we will not equate satisfaction with monetary status, but with the
status of our identity. The reason for this is that the "end" of our career phase
in life places us squarely in the experience of our own end.

Vocation
Lifework originates from a person's sense of vocation and is transferred through
a career strategy and supported through employability skills. The idea of making
money is subservient to making a life.

A vocation refers to the "calling" or more concretely the experiences that we genuinely and intuitively enjoy in life. Our sense of vocation compels us toward a sense of personal fulfillment and is intimately connected with our private narrative. A career is a chosen occupation and professional endeavor that originates in our economic circumstances. We can choose a career that is connected to our vocation in life, or our vocation in life may be realized through a hobby. In other words, our careers may or may not be connected to the things in life from which we derive personal fulfillment. Employability refers to how our skills and abilities are in economic demand and is more of a tactical and practical orientation to earning an income in order to achieve a desired lifestyle.

From a more critical perspective, the idea of employability in the absence of a meaningful career strategy forces us to lead a highly reactive life, especially in the face of persistent technological innovation and change. To ensure employability we constantly *upgrade* our skills so that we are able to make a viable contribution to a business enterprise. Further, a career strategy in the absence of a genuine understanding and pursuit of our vocation may lead to a life of economic reward that is disconnected from our source of enjoyment and fulfillment in life. In an ideal world, the economy would of course facilitate the complete integration of vocation, career, and employability. We do not live in an ideal world, but the pursuit of unity across these three domains is a fundamental direction and aim of learning.

The human quest for unity across vocation, career, and employability is captured in the word lifework.

Deciding what our lifework will be is one of the most important explorations we will undertake. It is a basic way in which we give direction to our private and public narratives, and is therefore an important means for giving ourselves an identity. Lifework is also directly connected to the hard realities of economic requirement. Not all vocations can be economically supported by a society, but this reality does not make them any less important. It is probably the quest to reduce the gap between vocation, career and employability that is the real foundation for what we refer to as *entrepreneurship*. At its most elemental and instinctual level, entrepreneurship is really a desire for identity.

The collision of personal identity with economic reality is the source of both opportunities and problems. When the gap between our sense of vocation and our career is wide, we enter into the world of psychological and emotional hazards, not the least of which are anxiety and depression. Our identity, in this circumstance, is literally ill. When the gap between our career strategy and the reality of employability is wide, we become highly reactive, stressed, and insecure in the face of a haphazard and somewhat schizophrenic working style. It is entirely possible to earn a high income, have a financially stress-free lifestyle and be unhappy; it is also entirely possible to earn a modest or low income, have a financially challenging lifestyle and be completely happy. Money and currency have no correlation with profit and contentment, except for those that have sadly linked their sense of happiness to their financial wealth.

The idea of lifework is to explore the ways and means in which people can bring a greater sense of coordination and unity to their vocation, career and employability. Earning an income is an unavoidable reality in a capitalistic society. Feeling personally fulfilled through the pursuit of a career is a basic human right in a democratic society. Pursuing one's bliss and calling in life in a universal human right. None of this is an ode to rampant individualism, self-centeredness and an irresponsible sense of personal entitlement. It is impossible to pursue one's vocation in the absence of being accountable and responsible to others. It is the relationship between our private and our public identity that is the ground for seeking unity. At the same time, modern societies demand that we make money in order to be able to provide the basic elements of survival (food, shelter, and clothing) as well as a reasonable lifestyle (entertainment, recreation, material possessions). Given the fact that we are required to earn an income for approximately forty years of our lives in order to survive in a capitalistic society, we need to ensure that these forty years have as much fulfillment as possible.

Lifework is one possible motivation for network learning environments and a purpose for exploration. It is one possible answer to the question, "Why am I exploring this learning environment?" Lifework makes an intimate connection to narratives and the development of private and public identities. It is a universal target for learning to take aim. Finally, lifework provides a more comprehensive and effective framework for the idea of *preparing people for the workplace*. Corporations literally connect the employee's identity to their *monetary value add*, or the employee's financial contribution to the business minus what they have to be paid (i.e. salary, benefits, expenses). This is what is often referred to as the *end of the day* or the *bottom-line reality* of the corporate experience. Of course, the obvious reality is that people need to find jobs and earn an income so they can support themselves. At the same time, people are far more than mere cogs in the economic machinery. If we think about our careers merely in terms of required skill sets needed to get a job then we are playing Russian roulette with our well being. There has been a great deal of progress made in the area of physical safety in the work environment, however there is now a great need for psychological safety in the workplace.

What are we really saying when we state that we need to *prepare people for the workplace*? What does the word *prepare* really refer to? Whose idea of *preparation* is it? What are the hidden assumptions and tacit conditions implied? As long as a capitalist filter prevails, we will all be faced with the bottom-line of a career life intimately connected with profits, revenues, balance sheets, contribution equated with cost—in other words, money. Education in this context has no *business* in the workplace, and the workplace has no business in education. If corporations require specific internal skill sets they should not be downloading them into public education.

Employability

The Conference Board of Canada's *Employability Skills 2000+* (www.conferenceboard.ca/nbec) is a baseline document outlining "The skills you need to enter, stay in, and progress in the world of work—whether you work on your own or as part of a team." The skill sets are divided into three categories: a) Fundamental Skills—communicate, manage information, use numbers, think and solve problems; b) Personal Management Skills—demonstrate positive attitudes and behaviors, be responsible, be adaptable, learn continuously, work safely; and c) Teamwork Skills—work with others, participate in projects and tasks. The *Employability Skills Toolkit* is aimed at helping individuals identify and improve upon skills that lead to desired employment opportunities. The creation of the document was based on input from fifty-three member organizations participating in two forums: a) the Employability Skills Forum; and b) the Business and Economics Forum on Science, Technology, and Mathematics. The underlying assumption is an agenda of improved national economic viability through the promotion of science and technology. The theme of *skills for the workplace* is a common symbol of the intersection between economic utility and education.

The underlying process is important to illuminate here. The document is the result of committees of representatives from various industry sectors in the Canadian economy. The underlying question is "What human assets does the Canadian economy require to remain viable in the global economy?" The headings *Fundamental Skills, Personal Management Skills,* and *Teamwork Skills* represent an organizer to consolidate the various ideas presented from the various member organizations. The result is a statement of requirements from the corporate sector, brokered by the government to the education and training sector. In other words, a great deal of analysis and thought was given to economic issues resulting in a de-contextualized, but somewhat useful, perspective on workplace perceptions and the implications for education and training.

It is a futile argument to suggest that education should *not* be accountable for preparing people for the workplace. To support an education system that does not do this in concrete terms is to support a system that alienates people from forty or more years of their lives. However, to limit the idea of education to the acquisition of skills that increase the potential of employability is not a strong enough foundation either. Employability cannot be given enough direction without being integrated with a viable perspective on career strategies and personal vocation. To master workplace skills in the absence of these higher elements is a recipe for rampant discontent in our society. At the same time, the acquisition of skills associated with the traditional subject discipline expertise that dominates education is equally inadequate preparation for the work place.

When the requirements of the workplace are transitory and malleable, preparation for the workforce often means to acquire highly generalized skill sets. Under the heading "Fundamental Skills" in the *Employability Skills 2000+* document we see four subheadings: a) Communicate; b) Manage Information; c) Use Numbers; and d) Think and Solve Problems. The skills under "Communicate" make general statements about reading, writing, listening, sharing, comprehending, and applying knowledge. The premise is that if a person can master these skills, they are prepared to communicate in the workplace and therefore are more employable. From an educational perspective, it is hard to imagine any subject area that could not accommodate these skill sets. Under the heading "Personal Management Skills" we see five subheadings: a) Demonstrate Positive Attitudes and Behaviors; b) Be Responsible; c) Be Adaptable; d) Learning Continuously; and e) Work Safely. To *be adaptable*, for example, means to have the ability to "carry out multiple tasks or projects" and to "cope with uncertainty." On the surface, this is a way of saying that we need to squeeze every last ounce of productivity out of ourselves. Finally, under the heading "Teamwork Skills" we see two subheadings: a) Work With Others; and b) Participate in Projects and Tasks—both underscored with generalized skill statements as in the previous two sections.

Indications about what people can expect in return from the workplace are often absent. The basic requirement of any economy is to be responsible to the people it embraces, and not merely be a vehicle for capitalistic growth and innovation. This point of intersection captures the needed convergence between the goals of education and the requirements of the economy.

The conditions of time in the new capitalism have created a conflict between character and experience, the experience of disjointed time threatening the ability of people to form their characters into sustained narratives. (Sennett, Richard 1999)

In the *Corrosion of Character*, Richard Sennett offers a true account of the lives and careers of Enrico and Flavia. In particular, Enrico suffers the effects of the slogan of the new economy, "No long term." The episodic nature of employment in a constantly shifting work environment creates emotional instability in people. Enrico goes on to say; "You can't imagine how stupid I feel when I talk to my kids about commitment. It's an abstract virtue to them; they don't see it anywhere." (Sennett, Richard 1999) Corporations typically commit less to people and more to the bottom line. We live this existence for long periods of time in our lives. Families have fewer models of commitment to draw from. Downsizing and divorce become synonymous.

It has become apparent, if not obvious, that there is a close correlation between anchoring ourselves in the economy and mental health. The Canadian Business and Economic Roundtable on Addiction and Mental Health reported that mental health and other stress related problems are costing Canadian businesses approximately $16 billion per year. This represents a total of 14% of the net income for all businesses in Canada. Depression is a leading cause of workdays lost to disability. These are *Hard Times* of a more profound nature. The Canadian Centre for Addiction and Mental Health concludes that:

6. Lifework

People with physical illness tended to take full days off. People with mental disorders were more likely to either go to work and leave early, or stay at work and struggle through the day.

"The number of partial work days and extra-effort days came to about two months per year per person with a mental disorder, compared to one month per year for a person with a physical illness." (Post, National 2001)

Further, one in ten Ontario adults report having a child under the age of eighteen with mental, emotional, or behavioral problems. Thirty-two percent indicated they knew of someone with a child in this situation. (Wright, John 2000) Uniformly equating people with abilities to access information and the performance of skill sets is a means to create uncertainty, paranoia, anxiety, depression, and discontent. The reasons for the decline of our emotional well being are not mysterious, nor can real improvements be made in this spiraling malady unless we are willing to question and evolve our underlying assumptions and mindsets. The development of "well being" seminars, emotional intelligence, and other mental health oriented programs are important, but will remain the equivalent of a prescription medication that lessens the effect of an illness, but does not deal with the cause.

If a person is to be considered *employable*, they need to possess more than mere skill sets. Highly intelligent people are often on the periphery of society in the sense that they do not necessarily accept the established norm and status quo. These are people that are often highly skilled and therefore employable in the narrowest sense of the term. They may be completely unemployable in every other sense of the term. The solution is to find higher ground against which to reference employment skills, so that the mastery of skill sets originates in the requirements of the corporation in balance with the individual career requirements of the real person under consideration. We need to educate people more effectively about career sensibilities; corporations need to take responsibility and be accountable to the career sensibilities of the people they employ.

The idea of *career sensibility* is an emergent property of networks. The above examples of employability skills, education practices, corporate practices, and mental health are key design elements. If we seek a transparent society, we will invite surveillance into the network in order to shed light on areas commonly thought of as being private. This might include here a complete openness toward: a) challenging the education system to account for direct and concrete connections between twelve years of subject discipline expertise and forty years of economic realities; b) challenging the corporation to be more responsible and accountable for their employees in terms of the career and vocation; c) demanding a reciprocal relationship between the imposition of required skill sets and the real return on investment in terms of one's career; and d) elevating the issue of human well being as being the most fundamental indicator of real profit.

Career Sensibility

A career is not the same thing as a job. In terms of foresight, a career represents a general path of experiences we would like to have over the course of our lives that also provides the kind of income we desire. In terms of hindsight, a career is the thing we look back upon to see what really happened while we were earning an income. When we place our foresight in the presence of hindsight we reflect upon our level of satisfaction with what we have done. In the face of death, we will not equate satisfaction with monetary status, but with the status of our identity. The reason for this is that the "end" of our career phase in life places us squarely in the sight of our own end. Death itself and how we come to it is the ultimate standardized test for all of us.

Consider that we are in the employability phase of our lives for approximately forty years. We spend roughly half of our lives predominantly through the filter of employment. We also spend approximately 20% of our lives in formal education. Taken together, this constitutes approximately 75% of our lives. A substantial portion of our lives is directed to preparing for and living through a career. This means that 75% of our lives, for most of us, is spent attempting to live up to imposed standards and criteria for success.

A wonderful article written by Harvey Schachter appeared in the April 1997 issue of Canadian Business, entitled *Forget the Suit, Get Me an Anvil*. The article described five case studies in which people abandoned corporate life in search of greater career satisfaction. Each person followed a pattern of outlining the nature of disillusionment with his or her corporate reality. The result was an instinctive and highly emotional need to change their life. Their personal narratives and identity were in conflict with their career paths. The career transitions these people created were: 1) from an investment-banker to a blacksmith; 2) from an advertising executive to a massage therapist; 3) from a human resources specialist with a bank to a furniture maker; 4) from a bank manager to a chef; and 5) from a supervisor of aerial survey teams to a trailer campground operator. In each case these people moved courageously from making things with their minds to making things with their heart and hands.

There are stories in the world that everyone would benefit from exploring.

This kind of career change is literally a mythological act of survival. Their personal commentary reveals their motivations:

CAREER TRANSFORMATIONS

HEART

Investment Banker to Blacksmith
The turning point came in 1987 when his father died of a brain aneurysm. "It stopped my mind," Huck says. "It showed me, so vividly, that death comes without warning and that I'd better start following my heart in life." Still, it took him two years to escape his career...

QUALITY

Advertising Executive to Massage Therapist
"In terms of quality of life and my health, I'm miles ahead with the switch," he says. "I can't imagine being this healthy if I stayed in advertising. The pace I was working at was too hectic, and there was no time to stop and smell the roses."

RISK

Human Resource Specialist to Furniture Maker
He had not developed a financial plan and is happy he didn't: "I am not sure it would have helped me. I did a lot of thinking about why I wanted to make this change, rather than how I would do it. I figured the money would follow."

SATISFACTION

Bank Manager to Chef
"I'm exploring something I have always been interested in doing. In 100 years, it won't matter that I ran a small cafe in St. Mary's. But I have helped make our customers satisfied. And that's deeply satisfying."

STABILITY

Aerial Survey Supervisor to Trailer Campground Operator
"It got to the point where I was probably spending 90% of my time out of the country," says Dick.... "I hadn't noticed how much of a pressure cooker the other job was until I left it."

While we might think of these simply as a form of discontent that led to a career change, this is an inadequate understanding of the power of learning at play here. These are exemplary narratives of lifework. Not only did each person make their career more *sensible*, they also developed a refined sense of awareness and appreciation of their personal identity in relation to the situations and circumstances in which they found themselves. The tacit conditions of stress and unhappiness that provide the underlying ground for each career change, or the *inevitable vale of tears*, provided the basis for personal empowerment. These are modern-day myths that are heroic in quality as well as essential experiences for others to survey. Abstract and over-generalized skill sets and models of career decision-making common to education and training environments are completely vacuous without these narratives. We cannot be truly prepared for the workforce unless they have stories like these in which to center themselves. Without narrative, we confine ourselves to rampant and dislocated career changes and psychological distress throughout our lives.

CAREER SENSIBILITIES

NARRATIVE

Each individual realized that their personal identity was suffering. The narrative they were living in their career and the narrative they desired were in conflict. A career, even a highly successful one, can make a person unhappy. To ask the question, "Why am I spending my life in this way and what needs to be done about it?" is fundamental to establishing a meaningful career sensibility.

ENVIRONMENT

Each individual literally took charge of designing their own experience, crafted a learning environment for themselves, planned an entirely new set of interactions, and embraced the emergent properties.

EXPLORATION

Each of these stories is an exemplar of human exploration originating in the question, "What should my career be?" The motivations are all intrinsic: a) the death of a father; b) the reclamation of health; c) personal reflection and assessment; d) the need for greater satisfaction; and e) a constant physical location and sense of home.

6. Lifework

In *Part One: Learning,* the limitations of traditional curriculum approaches were explored. The terms used to describe these limitations include mechanization, automation, fragmentation, and bureaucratization. The phrase *the primacy of information* was used as a general phrase to capture these limitations. The five examples of career sensibility above represent one possible modern life source of design for a curriculum that is designed to prepare people for the workplace. *Forget the Suit, Get Me an Anvil* is a source of inspiration and motivation for interaction design. The idea of career sensibility is a focus for developing the critical and creative vitality of exploration. The result is a vibrant network learning environment.

If there is something called an *entrepreneurial spirit,* these stories are also exemplary. The problem with entrepreneurship is that it is closely equated to innovation with respect to business directions in the absence of a guiding framework in which people can center their lives. If we are to be *entrepreneurial* then we are inviting a mythological career quest more than we are the possibility of economic profits. Money, as a source of motivation for a personal quest, can only lead to a poverty of the human spirit. The true examples of entrepreneurship are not the bright lights of return on investment. Return on investment is the source of "innovation" within the status quo. Regardless of economic power and influence, we each answer to the universal reality of death. Death is the essence and defining feature of life that positions all of us firmly in the grasp of the power of myth.

Looking back at the previous issue of *employability* we can now clearly see how the idea of *preparation for the workplace* as a set of abstract and over-generalized skill sets pales in the face of career sensibility. We have illuminated the glaringly obvious reality that highly skilled people can be highly discontent in their lives. The question, "Whose sense of employability is this and why should I believe it is of personal relevance to my career sensibilities?" is fundamental. The concept of preparation for employability through skill acquisition is a remnant of the primacy of information. Just as isolated subject disciplines in the education system fragment the experience of people into largely irrelevant categories, the acquisition of employability skills in the absence of a larger human purpose and framework fragments the experience of people in their careers.

Looking ahead to the idea of *vocation* we will explore how our intuitive sense of a personal calling is the source of design for a meaningful approach to career sensibilities and employability. It is vocation that most closely and intimately connects us to the core idea of the private and public narrative. Vocation is also the source of design for a profound orientation to a network learning environment, because the achievement of one's personal and individual vocation is never accomplished in the absence of other people. The issue of vocation is ultimately the emerging unification that occurs between private and public narratives; something completely new and unique emerges from the synergy between private and public interest.

Vocation

A vocation intimately connects us to our private and public narrative, the fundamental source of stability in learning. While not strictly limited to ideas about employment, careers, and economy, the word *vocation* is the point of origin for design. Lifework originates from a person's sense of vocation and is transferred through a career strategy and supported through employability skills. It is also here that we find the most profound opportunities for network learning environments and Exploration with respect to economic development.

The word *vocation* refers to an intuitive sense of being "called" to a particular profession or pursuit in life. In other words, it is an inclination for a person to engage in an occupation for which they are intellectually, emotionally, and spiritually well suited. We commonly think of a person being "called" to religion and their occupation in life lies within the church. But a vocation need not be centered in the divine or spiritual; anyone can feel a calling to a profession, occupation, or lifestyle. The apprehension of one's vocation is primarily a kind of felt meaning that is intuitive and that is a source of motivation for that person.

The common definition of the word *entrepreneur* is a person that has the courage and assumes the risk for creating and managing a business venture. One of the motivating forces of this may be improvement of one's economic circumstances, however, this is not a requirement. At its most basic level, entrepreneurship represents the interaction of business development with vocational pursuit. It is a means to *take control* of the narrative of our economic lives, a means to create more optimal environments for our career sensibilities, and most importantly a means to create identity. Entrepreneurship is the means to explain ourselves to ourselves through the filter of commerce.

Of course, there are many employability skills associated with entrepreneurship (e.g. writing a business plan, corporate law, accounting, operations and management, etc.), but these skills are a modest subset of a much larger psychological phenomenon.

Industry Canada identifies the mission of a *Smart Community* as using ICT (Information and Communications Technologies) in community or country to "create jobs and economic growth as well as improve the overall quality of life within their communities." (http://smartcommunities.ic.gc.ca). The phrase "improve the overall quality of life" is particularly notable as an aim for the effective application of networks. This value proposition of a Smart Community is enormous in magnitude. If we are to improve the quality of life in a community or country, then we are developing strategies for stability in the face of the confluence of modern life. From this point of view, a Smart Community is a means to explore how technology can benefit people. In the end, a Smart Community is a network learning environment that frames a community of practice as a kind of "learning laboratory" in order to identify best practices for the use of ICT.

The word *smart*, however, may not have been the best choice of words to characterize a community. As a reference to our intelligence a person is smart if we feel they are quick witted, clever, shrewd, and elegant in their thinking. The end result of a person's "smartness" may or may not be of benefit. History is filled with many dictators and criminals who we would consider to be smart. From a technological perspective, the word *smart* refers to machines that are considered to have a high degree of automation, even though everything they accomplish is limited to mathematical formulae. The "smart bomb," a technological symbol of the Gulf War, has a high degree of automation in the destruction of people, places, and things. A person can be smartly dressed, which means they possess a fashionable facade, but this has no correlation to the character beneath the fashion. If something "smarts" it is a source of pain. A comic oriented to sarcastic forms of humor is a kind of "smart ass." In each of these examples it is entirely possible for a person or group of people to be judged as *smart* regardless of their actions; many smart people do incredibly stupid things.

A *smart community* is an initial sketch of a *network learning environment*. In the first place, the aim of a smart community is to provide a kind of *learning environment* for people to *explore*. The learning environment is one that is intended to converge upon critical issues. I use the word *convergent* in its bio-logical sense: "The adaptive evolution of superficially similar structures, such as the wings of birds and insects, in unrelated species subjected to similar environments. In this sense, also called *convergent evolution.*" (*The American Heritage Dictionary of the English Language, Third Edition*, 1992). This is a different sense of *convergence* in comparison with its technological use (i.e. the combining of hardware and software into integrated devices and pro-grams). The *similar environment* or shared opportunity with respect to a community is learning. The *superficially similar structures* are corporations, governments, educational institutions and cultural organizations. A commu-nity is a collection and cross-representation of corporate, governmental, edu-cational, or cultural interests and needs that converge in an attempt to create a community of practice and public identity.

In the economic domain, the most important goal for a smart community is to provide a network learning environment that facilitates the convergent evolution of vocation, career, and employability. In any culture, people are unavoidably connected to similar structures, relationships and environments in their lives. The corporate structure seeks power through profit. The gov-ernment structure seeks power through elections. The educational structure seeks power through the rites of passage. The cultural structure seeks power through expression. The interaction of a person's vocation, career, and employability in the face of the societal motivations of profit, elections, certi-fication, and expression is fundamental to the creation of a smart commu-nity. The idea of convergent evolution means that as much as we think of people being "prepared" for society, the society is also "preparing" for them. The relationship between the individual and the existing power structures is reciprocal. Summarizing the required skill sets for economic success and broadcasting those skill sets to other societal structures is hardly a basis for a smart community since the direction of ideas and information is essentially one-way and emanates from one kind of expertise. The systemic require-ments of convergence, evolution, and adaptation are commonly ignored, resulting in the one-way production of documentation.

In a network learning environment, the various power structures still lever-age their expertise but the context of communication is transparent and under constant surveillance by all participants. For example, the education sector might prepare a requirements document for the other sectors that out-lines the vocational and career aspirations of our youth. Our tendency, of course, is to assume that education is preparatory in nature. There is no need or benefit in framing an education as a kind of preparation. The education sector is a smart community that has the power to inform other power structures. While the government-corporate sectors prepare their requirements documents, such as the *Employability Skills 2000+,* the education sector might prepare a requirements documents such as a *Human Vocational Demands 2000+.*

> *Any community that purports itself as being* smart *would not ignore the real aspirations and hopes of the people in that community. Any economy that would be seen as* viable *would not ignore the issue of* lifework.

For the Smart Community concept to evolve it first needs to challenge its underlying assumption. That assumption is that access to information is the basis for improving the quality of life. Access to information in no way improves the quality of anyone's life in any substantial way, nor does it by itself improve the conditions for learning. Even though the Smart Community concept is framed by networks, it is an application of traditional information design embodied by the Internet. A smart community must originate in the promotion of learning, not the dissemination of information.

> *Lifework is a work of art, and the art of work.*

Strategic Directions: Lifework

ELIMINATE TRANSIENT SETS OF COMPETENCIES AS A SOURCE OF DESIGN

The idea of being employable is far more complex and sophisticated than short-term solutions designed to provide generic competencies for all. Being proficient with current technology in no way guarantees being proficient at developing a career.

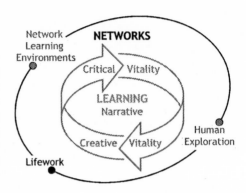

PROMOTE THE IDEA OF CAREER SENSIBILITY

The creation, management, and resolution of a person's career in society is a lifelong endeavor. As much as people need to be prepared for the workforce, the workforce must also prepare itself for people.

ELEVATE THE PURSUIT OF VOCATION IN LEARNING

A vocation is the place where our intuition speaks to us and guides us to satisfaction with the things we choose to do in our lives. Both our careers and employment need to support our vocational aspirations in a healthy society.

COLLECT AND DISSEMINATE EXEMPLARY NARRATIVES OF LIFEWORK

The provision of narratives that capture and elevate the pursuit of our vocation in life is the most important source of design for considering ideas about careers and employment.

PART THREE: THE CYBERSPHERE

Thought Process

The Cybersphere is the surrounding of electronic communications that take place through the Internet. It is an evolving matrix of computer networks that connect computers around the world.

The Cybersphere allows people and organizations to build electronic relationships with each other that are not limited by geographical distance. In many ways, our use of the Internet is a retrieval of traditional practices made digital— the governmental, corporate, educational, and cultural agendas are extended into this environment.

The ecology of the Cybersphere provides a variety of creative possibilities for learning. These creative possibilities originate in experience design. The future of e-Learning in the Cybersphere is clearly centered on how well we can integrate the authentic experiences of real people with the virtual experiences of the Internet.

Probes

! *E-Learning has yet to be invented. E-Learning is not the same as e-Education and e-Training.*

! *The design of the design process needs to be re-designed. Interface design, information architecture, and communications design are all subsets of experience design.*

! *The Internet is an electronically networked learning environment that consists of many kinds of electronic habitats, each with its own characteristics.*

! *The learner is not merely a user of tools, but a designer and creator of them. What users do with Internet tools is of far greater importance than how designers intend them to be used.*

! *The current industry practices of e-Learning are transient and fleeting—they do not provide a sustainable foundation for innovation and growth.*

! *Unless the e-Learning industry adopts a more comprehensive view of experience design, it is destined to mediocrity and eventually extinction. The loss of this potential represents a loss of global proportions.*

Overview

Chapter 7: e-Learning Habitats

If the Internet is a vast matrix of networks, then the most powerful designer of the Internet is the experience designer. A learner is as much a designer of e-Learning as they are a user of it. The vast majority of our current e-Learning habitats have little to do with learning, and a great deal more to do with education and training. The future of e-Learning is dependent upon how effectively we can lift ourselves out of traditional approaches to education and training and embrace a comprehensive approach to experience design.

The e-ffect
It is important to develop a clear understanding of the effect of placing the letter "e" in front of words such as learning. The grammar of learning and the grammar of e-Learning are not the same. The distinctions between the two are fundamental to the development of innovation and growth.

e-Habitats
An e-Learning habitat is a specific kind of network within the matrix of networks that comprise the Internet. The design and evolution of these electronic learning habitats is the shared responsibility of the learner and the designer.

Understanding e-Learning
The meaning, design, production, and value of e-Learning must be clearly understood in human terms. This forms the basis for examining how any software can be transformed into tools for e-Learning.

Chapter 8: Mindware

Mindware is a design strategy is aimed at empowering the learner to use software critically and creatively. The efficient use of software has little to do with the effective use of software. The expert learner will discover more effective uses for software than the original producers could ever hope to imagine.

The Software's Apprentice
The efficient use of software as a training goal has little relationship to the effective use of software to support learning. Mastering the skills required by software tools has no direct correlation with the mastery of learning. People do not become skilled learners merely by mastering the operation of software.

What is e-Learning Software?
The transformation of a software application into an e-Learning application is achieved through the process of Mindware. In spite of the fact that many companies have failed to identify and support the latent e-Learning potential in their products does not mean that the software cannot be used by the critical and creative learner as an e-Learning tool.

The Mindware Industry
The future development of e-Learning requires an integrated network of government, educational, corporate, and cultural enterprises for success. None of these sectors, on its own, possess the broad range of intelligence and experience required to lead a new e-Learning paradigm. The impact of this new paradigm is pervasive.

Chapter 9: e-Learning Design

The future of e-Learning technology requires a network learning environment that integrates the corporate, governmental, educational, and cultural sectors. The rationale for this is based on: a) no one sector has the necessary intelligence to evolve e-Learning to new levels of value and performance; b) learning is a source of design that transcends any one sector; and c) network technologies are most effectively developed by powerful, adaptive, and flexible networks of relationships.

Designing the Designers
The designers of e-Learning systems need to recalibrate their activities. To accomplish this, we need to prepare people for a career in e-Learning in a new way. It is not enough to be an expert designer in the absence of being an expert experience designer.

Designing the Experience
Interface design is abandoned for experience design; web architecture is abandoned for web experience; software programmers evolve to learning engineers. The gap between the people building learning tools for use on the Internet and the people that actually use them is reduced.

The Experience of e-Learning
The Experience Designer is a foundation for schools, colleges, and universities to modify existing programs as well as to create entirely new programs. With respect to the Internet, new media designers that are expert in experience design will provide leadership for not only a new e-Learning paradigm, but a new paradigm for learning itself.

7. E-LEARNING HABITATS

The most important design consideration for e-Learning is to think of it as a unique kind of electronic habitat within the more comprehensive idea of a *network learning environment.* An e-Learning environment is primarily designed to facilitate *human ingenuity.*

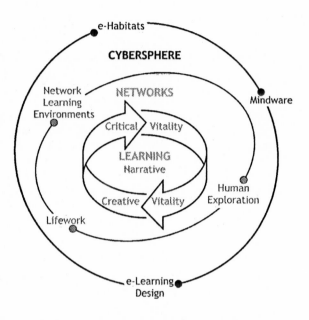

How can the idea of e-Learning be restructured in order to promote more innovative and creative approaches to learning?

The use of old education and training paradigms within new technological environments is, unfortunately, a well established norm. E-Learning has been needlessly reduced to ways of delivering information and traditional course structures on-line. In intellectual and economic terms, this approach is not sustainable.

Chapter Design

The e-ffect
It is important to possess a clear understanding of the effect of placing the letter "e" in front of words such as learning in order to clarify the grammar of both learning and e-Learning.

e-Habitats
An e-Learning habitat is a kind of electronically networked space designed to facilitate exploration, discovery, and invention.

Understanding e-Learning
The ability to constantly clarify what can and cannot be accomplished in e-Learning systems is fundamental to its effectiveness.

A *habitat* is a specific kind of area that is part of a larger environment. In a habitat we find systems of communities that have a particular character and quality. For example, in the natural environment we refer to a variety of habitats including the rain forest, the desert, a coral reef, a forest, the grasslands, and many more. An environment is something that surrounds and envelops a habitat. For example—wind systems, precipitation, temperature, climatic patterns, and pollution are all environmental elements that directly affect and provide the conditions that surround a habitat.

> *Understanding that* e-Learning *is a specific kind of habitat within a larger system of* learning *is a critical design principle.*

The term "e-Learning" is plagued by confusion, controversy, and distortion, while at the same time it is being ordained as the next wave of innovation in the technology sector. Its real value in the "human" sector remains unknown. In its current form and function, e-Learning is not so much an opportunity or solution to anything; it is a problem to be solved. The technology sector is racing into the digitization of past practices at blindingly efficient speed, all under the banner of *innovation*. Further, the kinds of assumptions, biases, and cognitive distortions emanating from this competitive race to intensify and accelerate the old through the new are leaking into other sectors in society. Most notably, status quo traditions of training, education, and learning are being perpetuated.

How can we come to a useful understanding of the term "e-Learning?" What does e-Learning as a habitat within a larger environmental system really mean? Why use metaphors from the natural environment to try to bring a better sense of understanding to environments that are exclusively mathematical-logical? These critical questions and others are of immediate relevance at a societal level. The power of e-Learning to produce bad results is at least equal to its ability to promote good results.

> *Human learning will always make e-Learning look like a rounding error.*

The dominant purpose of training in the workplace is to spend the least amount of time and money to make employees more efficient and effective at their jobs. E-Learning is a substantial market opportunity. As an $815 billion expenditure (all figures are in U.S. currency), education and training represent the second largest sector of the U.S. economy behind healthcare. The market growth potential for e-Learning in K-12 schooling is estimated at $1.3 billion in 2001 to $6.9 billion in 2003. Similarly, the market growth potential for tertiary education is estimated at $1.2 billion in 2001 to $7 billion in 2003. Not surprisingly, the biggest growth is projected in the corporate e-Learning market space; the market growth here is estimated at $1.1 billion in 2001 to $11.4 billion by 2003. Finally, the global e-Learning market space is estimated at $300 billion in 2001 to $365 billion by 2003. (TechKnowLogia 2001) The reason for this trend is the expectation that training is perceived to be a solution to the problem of continual corporate reinvention and adaptation in order to survive. There are three basic problems with current practices in e-Learning design:

E-LEARNING DESIGN PROBLEMS

RETRIEVAL

Old Practices in a New Medium
The intensification of traditional approaches to course design, curriculum, administration, and testing are not useful assumptions for the design of e-Learning.

FUNCTIONS

E-Learning Software Embeds the Wrong Assumptions
The development of monolithic software applications (i.e. learning management systems, course authoring tools, etc.) for e-Learning represents a creative roadblock to innovation.

AUTHENTICITY

Lack of Systemic Integration
The promise of e-Learning as a means to improving access to learning has a very narrow kind of utility, and often serves to make our experiences increasingly simulated.

The focus of *Part Three: The Cybersphere* is on a specific electronic domain of experience. E-Learning is not a software product, but a design perspective on how we use all of the electronic potential of the Cybersphere.

The e-ffect

The first challenge is to understand the effects and significance of the adjective "e." The term *e-Learning* expands to *electronic learning*, or learning that is mediated by electronic technologies. If we were to be quite literal in the interpretation of this term, we could only conclude that it is completely nonsensical and degrading. Learning does not occur in electricity, unless we are somehow making a reference to the neural firing that takes place in the human brain. This means that learning is a human form and function that has no direct electronic or technological analogue. *Nor does there need to be one.* However, the commercialization of the term *e-Learning* makes us assume that learning does in fact take place in the guts of technology. It does not.

None of this is to say that there is not an important relationship between the human form and function of learning and the electronic habitat of the Internet. The fundamental source of design for something we might refer to as an *e-Learning habitat*, however, originates in human form and function and does not originate in software programming. In fact, this is the premise and bias that guides the design of this book and provides the rationale for first understanding *learning*, then investigating the relationship of learning to *networks*, and finally arriving at a design perspective for e-Learning in the cybersphere.

The use of the letter "e" and therefore the adjective *electronic* in front of the word *learning* specifies a particular kind of habitat that is completely surrounded and immersed in the total environment of the plethora of ways people learn. The immediately visible components of this habitat are physically constructed through the use of computer screens, speakers, keyboards, and microphones that are networked with and without wires to web servers. What we see on the computer screen, what we hear through the computer speakers, what we type on a computer keyboard, and what we say into the computer microphone are uniformly controlled by a mathematical-logical process called *computer programming*. This means that the e-Learning habitat itself is a mathematical language for the electronic simulation of specific kinds of experiences. In many ways, the art of the computer programmer and interface designer is to craft visual and auditory experiences that hide this inexorable connection to an underlying ground of mathematics. The words *electronic* and *digital* have a very clear and unavoidable connection to experiences that are driven by the logic and language of numbers.

The value of this is in understanding that e-Learning is a kind of digitally networked habitat that is designed to simulate experiences electronically through an underlying ground of mathematical programming routines. The nature of the simulation interfaces our eyes to a screen, our ears to a speaker, our hands to a keyboard, and our voices to a microphone. Our eyes see text, graphics, and animations. Our ears hear sound files and audio streaming. Our fingers tap on a QWERTY keyboard to create letters, words and sentences on the screen. Our voices speak to create text or to communicate over voice IP. Commonplace cutting edge innovations in the technology sector are linking our noses to digital scent devices, and our bodies to electronic body suits. Perhaps our tongues will eventually be interfaces with the mathematics of taste. In other words, our sense perception itself becomes conditioned and attuned to digital simulations. The idea of simulation is dominated by the idea of visualization, or a habitat that is dominated by our sense of sight and only secondarily by sound.

The design potential of e-Learning lies in two interrelated systems of thought: a) how genuine and authentic experiences can be effectively metamorphosed into electronic habitats; and b) how human sense perception can be effectively extended to and through the cybersphere in order to facilitate learning. Current thought and practice in the commercial field of e-Learning is more focused on the creation of courses and management systems for education and training. In other words, what is commonly referred to in the industry as *e-Learning* would be far better categorized as *e-education* and *e-training* since the actual source of design emanates from past practices of the industrial era. The reality of e-Learning today is still surrounded by the environment of bureaucratization, mechanization, and automation. Our traditional concepts of curriculum and instruction have not evolved and adapted to the potential of new electronic habitats. The reason for this is clear and not in any way mysterious: we have *not* originated our thinking from the most genuine and original source of design—the human environment we know as *learning*.

THE HIDDEN ASSUMPTIONS OF E-LEARNING

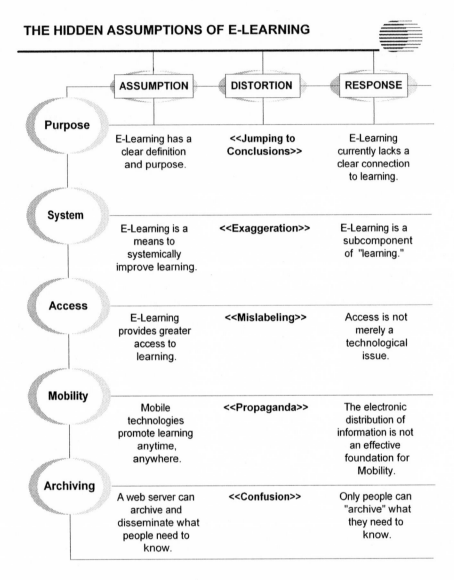

	ASSUMPTION	DISTORTION	RESPONSE
Purpose	E-Learning has a clear definition and purpose.	<<Jumping to Conclusions>>	E-Learning currently lacks a clear connection to learning.
System	E-Learning is a means to systemically improve learning.	<<Exaggeration>>	E-Learning is a subcomponent of "learning."
Access	E-Learning provides greater access to learning.	<<Mislabeling>>	Access is not merely a technological issue.
Mobility	Mobile technologies promote learning anytime, anywhere.	<<Propaganda>>	The electronic distribution of information is not an effective foundation for Mobility.
Archiving	A web server can archive and disseminate what people need to know.	<<Confusion>>	Only people can "archive" what they need to know.

The problem is that we have damaged the potential of e-Learning design with an array of psychological pollution. An erosion of the human sensibilities is occurring at a dramatic pace as they become more and more conditioned to e-Learning as a total environment rather than it properly being thought of as a habitat subsumed by a much larger and more powerful human system. The proliferation of control systems such as the LMS (learning management system), the EPSS (electronic performance support system), and on-line courseware authoring tools (e.g. WebCT) represent innovative retrievals of past practices embedded in long standing traditions of education and training. They are innovative only in the sense of offering variations on past practice. The level of collective distortion that occurs on mass level is substantial.

Cisco Systems Inc. (www.cisco.com) has developed the notion of a RLO (Reusable Learning Object) Strategy. "Cisco Systems recognizes the need to move from creating large and inflexible training courses to database objects that can be reused, searched, and modified independent of their delivery medium." Each RLO is created from RIO's (Reusable Information Objects). "An RIO is a granular, reusable chunk of information that is media independent. An RIO can be developed once, and delivered in multiple delivery mediums." The article goes on to say that *educational objects, learning objects, content objects, training components, nuggets,* and *chunks* are other ways of saying the same thing. In simpler terms, an RLO may be a lesson or activity and the facts and data that combine to create those lessons and activities are a collection of RIOs. So a bunch of RIOs (also known as *educational objects, learning objects, content objects, training components, nuggets,* and *chunks*) are combined make RLOs which in turn makes units which flow into topics that combine to create courses that are distributed on the web and lead to certification. It is difficult to imagine a more electronically bureaucratic and mechanized approach to education and training than this.

None of this is to say that the idea of RLOs and RIOs could not be useful, but it is to say that none of this really has much to do with learning. What becomes *reusable* in this strategy is the human being found guilty of the desire to learn. The ability to re-combine or possibly improvise with these objects does create a new sense of *play* in the construction of education and training experiences. Facts and information formerly confined to uniform curriculum classification, such as we see in school systems, are given more opportunity to interact with ideas in other categories in a kind of jazz ensemble approach to course design. In fact, for this technological design to be useful to learning, the individual controlling the content of the objects will have to be the learner. Doubtless to say, a learner is not going to want to create a course, they would rather learn.

The alphabet, the basis for intelligence itself, is a far more powerful example of RIOs and RLOs. Without the alphabet these objects could not exist. For that matter, we could consider print to be another kind of RLO. It was probably Gutenberg more than anyone else who invented the concept of RLO, even though he never used the term. Even a bad book is at the least a kind of reusable information object that can be reused, searched and modified. This use of our intelligence, even though slower than reusing, searching, and modifying objects digitally, has a far greater impact on how we learn. When we reuse, search, and modify our understanding of experiences and ideas using our brains, we are far closer to what learning is in comparison to digital simulation. It is interesting to consider the notion of "tagging" objects. The idea is to identify the intended use of an object by giving it a set of attributes. For example, Cisco's guidelines indicate that "based on the table above (i.e. the cognitive taxonomies of Merrill and Bloom), an Author will tag each RIO, or more specifically each learning objective as either *Remember* or *Use.* If the Author tags a learning objective as *Use,* then they will add a tag based on Bloom's taxonomy." For the purposes of this discussion, it is not important to understand either taxonomy.

A *tag* is an attribute in a database that is intended to point toward an intellectual capacity. With respect to learning, however, it is far more important that the learner *tags* information in relation to their own experience. This idea of tagging is quite a familiar one. A book comes to us with tags created by the author—these are commonly known as a Table of Contents, footnotes, appendices, and indices. If we are reading a book with vigilance, we commonly *tag* the book with a highlighter and a pen (i.e. add our own notes). We may even insert a torn-out section from a related magazine article, and other books. We may add a cross-reference from one part of the book to another that is not found in the indices. We may cross-reference a section of one book to a section of another. We may also enter into a conversation with other people who have also read the same book, but have *tagged* it in a different manner. In fact, the book is rich in opportunities for *tagging*, although we do not commonly teach this approach to reading.

> **A digital artifact will contain a list of imposed tags, but the human mind will always play tag with ideas and experience. Learning does not occur in databases—it occurs in people.**

This technological approach to the idea of *tagging experience* has some amusing side effects. Cisco indicates that the "concept" of a *cat* may be built as a reusable information object. In order to teach the concept of a *cat* through an information object, three kinds of items are required: a) content items—introduction, definition, facts, example, nonexample, analogy, instructor notes; b) practice items; and c) assessment items. The end result is that the learner is able to answer the question, "What is a cat?" The only possible answer, of course, is that a cat is a reusable information object that has a type of content, practice, and assessment written by an instructional designer. Other examples cited include horse, computer, hub, router, and switch. More importantly, this is an example of how easily the idea of learning becomes seduced by mathematical hallucinations and illusions.

e-Habitats

In order to illuminate the idea of e-Learning as a kind of habitat, three examples of e-Learning habitats are explored: a) e-Retrieval—the traditional practices of education and training mislabeled under the heading of e-Learning; b) EduCommerce—the convergence and alignment of marketing strategies with educational strategies; and c) Edutainment—a endangered idea that may have value in retrieving in the light of a new perspective on e-Learning.

Habitat 1: e-Retrieval

The divine e-Trinity of our time is e-Commerce, e-Business, and e-Learning. The letter "e," assumed to mean "electronic," has joined the ranks of prefixes that were fathered by the idiom of hyper-activity. The use of the letter "e" as a prefix is to indicate kinds of commerce, business, and learning that takes place by virtue of electronic network technologies. Even though we have electronic firings taking place in our brains, we do not tend to think of that as e-Learning. The light bulb is the most common and profound example of an electronic network technology, or e-Learning technology. The telephone and television would be further examples of this. E-Learning is invited into digital electronic networks through convergence—or the transference of existing technologies into a digital form and function.

We could say that *e-Learning* lacks any useful meaning since electricity cannot learn. We make the tacit assumption that we mean a kind of learning that occurs with the support of electronic technologies. The fundamental problem with this term "e-Learning" is that it uses a technology (electricity) to characterize a uniquely human capability (learning). This is compounded by the fact that most e-learning products have very little to do with learning and nearly everything to do with education and training. Of course, we should never assume that the label for something has anything to do with what it really is. We could, however, clarify a great deal of our confusion around e-Learning by giving it a label that is closer to its own reality. That reality is e-Training Courses, or to go further back in time, computer-based training (CBT) courses. The fact that e-Learning systems are driven by things like a LMS (Learning Management System) only intensifies the argument that current e-Learning practices have little to do with learning.

Corporations are embracing learning as a strategy for economic survival. E-Learning is the symbol of revitalization and innovation in the business world. Inside the corporation, learning is increasingly being seen by employees as a means to remain up-to-date, and therefore employable. The language of e-Learning is surrounded by workplace productivity metaphors, for example, *performance-based learning*. Traditional *bricks and mortar* training facilities as a physical location for training have given way to the electronic distribution of training via e-Learning. The false hope is seductively simple; e-Learning saves time and money, improves the quality of worker performance, and speeds up the productivity of the workforce. It is strategy for increasing the speed, scale, and dissemination of information *in just the right amount in just the right place at just the right time.*

There are four basic themes in techno-corporate edu-speak. The first is increased *access*, or the ability for learners to access "learning" through computers regardless of their geographic location. The second theme is increased *speed*, or the ability to disseminate "learning" more efficiently. A third is *money*, or the promise of reduced costs for learning. The fourth theme is the screen itself, or the obvious fact that e-Learning is intimately tied to things taking place on a computer screen. What is really becoming easier to access, faster, costing less money and presented on a screen are bits and bytes of up-to-date information often in the form of a course. Each of these associations originates from an underlying premise of an imaginary technological benefit rather than human potential. In this sense the e-Learning value statement is not a learning proposition but an information deposition.

The initial form and function of early attempts at e-Learning technology resembled the traditional course structures common to training and education. Our first attempts at e-Learning have retrieved the older print paradigm of curriculum design and delivery. Since the push of digital technology is toward the atomistic—or thinking increasingly in terms of many smaller elements—the content of topics and lessons become smaller and smaller objects and elements. In biology, we might refer to these as nits and mites, but in technology they are bits and bytes. Following the reductionist plot line, a course or lesson is ultimately broken down to its atomistic level, allowing it to be repurposed and recombined with the atomic elements from other courses and lessons. In other words, the digital reality of e-Learning becomes more oriented to the pieces and parts than to complete ideas, sustained thought and authentic experience.

Habitat 2: EduCommerce

When two previously remote aspects of society are suddenly connected through insight, we often see the birth of a new compound word. In the early days of multimedia, many words were appended with the prefix "hyper." We have already seen the birth and death of "edutainment" or the integration of education and entertainment. One of the more recent blindingly obvious insights is "edu-commerce" or the sudden collision of education and commerce. What this means is that brand identity is created and sustained through educational experiences in which people have a higher degree of interaction and participation in comparison with the advertising experience. Advertising is now a subset of education.

"EduCommerce" is defined as "the use of online education to develop deeper customer relationships, inspire greater brand loyalty, and drive bottom line revenues." (www.powered.com) The aim of the approach is to break new ground in Internet marketing. This approach to "sellers educating consumers" is exemplified by the bookseller Barnes and Noble (www.barnesandnoble-univeristy.com). The core idea is simple—use an online university concept to sell books. On the opening web page, the caption reads, "We have combined your passion for knowledge with our love of books, music, software, and video to bring you the future in learning." Consumers are attracted to purchasing books through the offer of participating in on-line courses "free of charge." The retailer is acting as a broker between the customer base and the

155

creator of or an expert on the products being sold. The expert is an on-line personality.

As an example, one of the free courses offered is about J.R.R. Tolkien's *The Hobbit* and *The Lord of the Rings*. The course instructor is a Ph.D. in Folklore and Mythology Studies, as well as a successful author. The course is seven weeks and four days in length. The requisite course materials are a boxed set of Tolkien's books in paperback at $36.00 USD. Eight other books are recommended to "enhance the learning experience" at a total cost of approximately $145.00 USD. If the consumer were to purchase all of these materials, the "free" on-line course would then cost approximately $181.00 USD. The instructor, undoubtedly expert in her field, also plays the role, even if indirectly, of sales representative. If one hundred people take the course and purchase one-third of the potential recommended resources on average, the course would generate approximately $6000.00 USD in sales. Additional marketing power is gained through the release of the movie series *Lord of the Rings,* beginning on December 19, 2001 with *The Fellowship of the Rings* (www.lordoftherings.net). This is an excellent approach to marketing as the buyer is given a great range of flexibility in deciding what to purchase. It is a different relationship from traditional course fees in which what might be considered recommended resources are in fact required.

Of course, this "sales" dimension of teaching is not uncommon or in opposition to what teachers or trainers do in schools and corporations. The school or training curriculum often needs to be sold to students, since the students are usually struggling to find relevance in it. In a school, however, the sales pitch is designed to build motivation to acquire the information the curriculum recommends. Publishers sell textbooks to support the requirements of the curriculum. In EduCommerce, the sales pitch is designed to build motivation to acquire the additional resources the company recommends. In one system, information is marketed and sold, and in the other, products are marketed and sold. Further, there is really no contradiction between spending money on the additional resources recommended for the course and the educational experience being provided. If the individual values this experience, then their money is "well spent."

Education is a commodity and a marketing strategy to sell products. For the consumer, the promise of EduCommerce is to give them a deeper experience into the product. In the case of Barnes and Noble, education is a value-added proposition to a book. This education is closely tied to the purchase of the "recommended" materials. Further, the Barnes and Noble brand identity is now enhanced through the provision of the "On-line University." Since it is web-based, the dissemination of this brand becomes viral in its capacity. The mass psychology of the consumer is captured and the critical objective for any brand—to create desire, need, and want—is fulfilled. Integrating the educative experience with the sales and marketing process is a powerful strategy for corporate survival, and is also an interesting value proposition to the consumer. The potential buyer at least has absolute authority over whether they choose to spend their money or not. The student in a classroom has no comparable power base with respect to the things they are being told they need to learn and the books they are required to read.

EduCommerce is an emergent example of how products can leverage education as a network marketing strategy. While its basic aim is to increase return on investments for a company, it also begins to further blur the traditional distinctions and social structures around education. This is a new age of "private schooling" and will have a deeper penetration into society than the current debates over public versus private education. Any organization can offer learning to either its consumers, business partners, or employees.

What is most important in all of this is the increased blurring of boundaries between the traditional and emerging social structure we refer to as "education." EduCommerce is a successful example since the concept was correctly built on the product being sold to the consumer. In both cases, two "different" industries converged. This is the most basic force with which education is faced—networks encourage the convergence of previously isolated sectors that lead to the creation of hybrid forms that give rise to new structures and processes of doing things.

If a bookseller can embrace education practices and integrate them into a sound business plan, then there is little reason why other companies could not do the same. A DVD player has wonderful potential for an edu-commerce strategy by establishing e-Learning communities around real movies that we really see in everyday life. Currently, most additional content on a DVD is of mild interest at best—there does seem to be a creativity crisis here. In a sense, if violence in the media is an issue, an integrated educational experience with the actual movie itself can serve at least as a buffer. Censorship of violent content would remain valuable, but it will have a companion in education. If it is impossible to avoid the bombardment of negative imagery in our lives, then edu-commerce may in fact be an ideal solution. Of course, this requires a much higher level of responsibility and accountability on the part of the media industry, but it is one they should not ignore. If a company can be profitable while helping people to find a center in the onslaught of media, then everyone profits. At the same time, the company will learn more about the cultural imagery it is producing and become more sensitive to its effects on people.

Edu-commerce means that the sole ownership and possession of education is no longer the sole province of the government. It also means that the public and private schooling debate, while important, is only a part of a much larger issue. The benefit that may come from a sensitive approach to the integration of education into commercial experiences can be a very substantial change agent for a culture. Of course, if education is reduced to a strategy merely for the purpose of making a profit, then it is reduced to a form of conditioning.

Habitat 3: Edutainment

The notion of "edutainment" failed to impact education since the idea was flawed from the outset. If the underlying field of information lacks relevance, then no amount of entertainment value will help sustain it over time. Like any good movie, there still needs to be a good story. Edutainment systems were designed to incorporate more entertaining features into existing curricular content in an attempt to make it more entertaining. The source of design—the education curriculum—was assumed to have value. An inversion of this approach would be more beneficial. The idea is better focused on incorporating more educational features into existing entertainment media. This means that the entertainment we already have, whether it be films, videos, television, music, or games, serves as the source for designing more interactive and entertaining forms of education.

A great deal of time and effort has been given to the on-going debate and opposition between educational practices and economic utility. An education that is limited to the external requirements of economic utility can correctly be viewed as a problem. At the same time, an education that is ignorant of the external requirements of economic utility is also correctly viewed as a problem.

People watch a lot of movies. How can a movie become the basis for learning? This question invites us to explore connections between the entertainment industry and education. From a technological perspective, the DVD player and interactive television are opportunities for education. From an educational perspective, movies are pervasive in people's experiences and therefore provide a very practical and relevant reference to everyday life. The integration of e-Learning into DVD technology results in an environment for virtual discovery. The movie is not translated into a course of study, but a cultural and technological artifact that is to be excavated through learning. From a technological perspective, the interactive capabilities of the media provide a rich toolset that can allow people to design learning experiences. Social issues such as the apparent connection between images of violence and occurrences of violent behavior might serve as a theme to extend the movie-watching experience into social activism. There is really nothing inherently wrong at all in thinking about a school as an educational version of a video store, as long as the quality and character of that education are primary.

The *edutainment* industry failed at this because it was based on applying entertainment to bland educational content. The premise was wrong even though the supporting logic made sense. The real content is the existing content produced by the entertainment industry itself, not the content produced by education systems. Education should be brought to entertainment. If education can profit by helping people understand the experiences that they will unavoidably have, whether in a school or not, then they become profitable. If entertainment can profit by creating products that embed e-Learning then they become profitable. In this context, there is no contradiction between entertainment and education. Of course, not all movie experiences need to be e-Learning experiences. I am imagining a critical mass of movie content that has critical value in the education of people. Further, the last thing we want to do is to create traditional courses around movies.

To explore the effects of violence in the media through a single movie, a cross-disciplinary team of movie producers, educators, social psychologists, government policy makers, victims of violence, concerned parents, and the like would need to be engaged. The result would not be a course but a comprehensive network environment. We can apply a similar approach to other pervasive digital environments such as e-games, e-zines, e-news, e-books, and e-mail. The underlying demand implied here is an echo of David Brin's idea of the *Transparent Society* (Brin, David 1998) and recalls the theme of learning as a means to undertake surveillance. E-Learning demands transparency and openness in our society and is a concrete environment for dealing with the issues and challenges of public versus private life.

Understanding e-Learning

UNDERSTANDING E-LEARNING

Meaning

The term *e-Learning* is really a nonsensical convergence of electricity with learning. *E-Learning* is useful if it is understood as the provision of an electronic habitat that exists within the larger system of the human phenomenon we call *learning*.

Design

The source of design for e-Learning originates in the human form and function of learning as it relates to a broad conception of networks. Current design practices in e-Learning are over-emphasizing technological innovation at the expense of sustainable value.

Production

The commercial enterprise of e-Learning is moving at a much faster pace than the human enterprise of learning. Current practices in e-Learning are retrievals of industrial-age practices in education and training. As an industry, e-Learning is mired in an unsustainable cycle of using the new to do the old.

Value

The language we use to describe the phenomenon of learning is the first and foremost requirement for the development of a new vision for e-Learning in the government, corporate, education and cultural sectors.

E-Learning is an idea rich in untapped potential.

The key to the development of innovative and visionary practices in e-Learning requires a creative analysis of the potential for all software to be used in a manner to support learning. What results is an emerging perspective on e-Learning through the transformation of how even basic productivity software applications can be used in innovative ways. Somewhat enigmatically, the software that we normally associate with e-Learning (e.g. courseware authoring tools, on-line courses, etc.) does not provide the best material for thinking about learning. In the end, effective e-Learning tools are as much about how people choose to use them as they are the technological sophistication of the software. In fact, technological sophistication and expensive software tools *are in no way a requirement* for the future of e-Learning. This approach is clarified in the next chapter.

Strategic Directions: e-Habitats

ELIMINATE CURRENT PRACTICES OF E-LEARNING AS E-EDUCATION AND E-TRAINING

The opportunity to elevate e-Learning beyond its current confines cannot occur unless a critical mass of people reach beyond the current paradigm of using new technologies to further entrench old ideas.

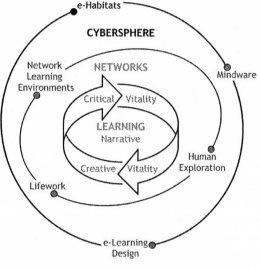

PROMOTE THE CREATION OF DIVERSITY IN E-LEARNING

Transfer the capacity to design and implement e-Learning into the hands of the learner. This means that the learner will be actively engaged in the design and use of their own personalized e-Learning tools and habitats.

DISTINGUISH THE GRAMMAR OF E-LEARNING FROM THE GRAMMAR OF LEARNING

The two ideas are rife with confusion, especially through the use of metaphors originating in a human ability that is later applied to a technological system. Both are important on their own terms.

COLLECT AND DISSEMINATE EXEMPLARY NARRATIVES OF E-LEARNING HABITATS

The provision of narratives that capture and clarify the unique qualities of various e-Learning habitats and how people actually make use of them leads directly to the discovery of new potential and opportunities.

8. MINDWARE

E-Learning is dependent upon the critical and creative vitality we bring to our use of Internet technology. A way of using networked software is first and foremost a creative act rather than a technical act with respect to learning.

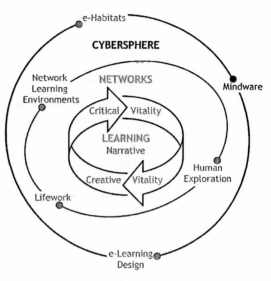

> **What is the most effective use of software to support learning?**

The production of such software entities as learning management systems, reusable information objects, and courseware authoring systems are all built on a transient set of assumptions. These modern day software development initiatives are examples of how new technologies can further entrench old paradigms of thought.

Chapter Design

The Software's Apprentice
Software has the power to coerce us into specific patterns of activity. Mindware is a thought process designed to counter-act this form of digital terrorism on the Internet.

What Is e-Learning Software?
Any software application can be transformed into an e-Learning application. This includes a traditional software application such as word processing as well as emerging technologies such as e-Books.

The Mindware Industry
E-Learning is currently under attack. Our initial tendency to embed traditional education and training practices is not the foundation for the future development of e-Learning.

The development and use of e-Learning software tools are the shared responsibilities of the designer and the user. The idea of e-Learning as a kind of course that is taken on-line is a smaller subset within this larger range of possibilities. The object of attention for both the software designer and the e-Learner is to find ways of unifying a wide repertoire of software tools into a unified system for learning. Mindware is a way to think about Internet software in these terms.

MINDWARE: TWO CRITICAL PERSPECTIVES

DESIGN

The design of hardware and software tools for e-Learning originates in the need to support human ingenuity. The design process of the tools themselves become the shared domain of both the designer and the user. The designer is as much a learner and the end user is. The critical point is that the learner is empowered to affect the design for him or herself at the level of software functionality. Courseware authoring tools, learning management systems, and resueable learning objects do not provide a liberating structure for mindware.

USE

The ways in which hardware and software tools are effectively used emanates from the human capacities of critical and creative vitality. This means that the mastery of skills required to operate hardware and software is not equated and often not relevant with respect to their effective use in learning. From the perspective of effective use, the idea of e-Learning as a kind of electronic habitat means that everyone in that habitat is simultaneously a designer, receiver, producer and participant in a manner that impacts the conditions for learning. More simply, the responsibility and accountability for content (i.e. information, knowledge, ideas) and process (individual and collaborative) are completely and evenly distributed to everyone. This means that e-Learning as a means to broadcast a pre-requisite content and process through a web server to the receiver, or students, of that content is no longer a predominant paradigm. In contrast, the one-way distribution of content, process and evaluation through a network that characterizes much of e-Learning today gives way to a more inclusive environment in which the learner also has the power of imposition over content, process and evaluation.

The Software's Apprentice

Yes, I have tricks in my pocket. I have things up my sleeve. But I am the opposite of a stage magician. He gives you illusion that has the appearance of truth. I give you truth in the pleasant disguise of illusion. (Tennessee Williams, The Glass Menagerie, 1945)

One definition of the word *tool* refers to a device that is designed to facilitate work. We may also refer to *tools for learning* or *learning tools*. It is important to remember, however, that the kinds of tools we use to accomplish industrial kinds of work are those that are largely extensions of our hands and legs. The kinds of tools we use to accomplish learning are largely extensions of our minds. Of course, both kinds of tools may have a role to play in learning, however, a hammer is a much different kind of tool than a word processor. The Internet is a vast playground of tools for learning.

Another definition of the word *tool* is in reference to a person that unknowingly carries out the desires of another. In this sense, a person that is labeled a *tool* has committed an act of ignorance in the sense that they really did not understand the implications of what they did. This act of stupidity is a reference to a lack of awareness and an unquestioning attitude toward the successful completion of imposed instructions and rules. The idea that technology is merely a *tool be used* and has value as an end unto itself originates in an act of ignorance. For example, there is nothing intrinsically important in a word processor. It is entirely possible to master word processing techniques and routines and thereby master the ability to write more and more about less and less. Learning word processing only to become better at word processing is a waste of time.

Mindware forces us to first ask the question: What is the larger purpose for which I am learning this software tool?

It is of fundamental importance to first understand how a software tool fits into the broader and more comprehensive issues of the individual and collective learning needs. Not only will this "big picture first" perspective help to contextualize the tool in a meaningful way, it will also determine what aspects of the software are more important than others. The completely unrewarding activity of learning all possible software functions in a training program is avoided and valuable time is saved. To say that *technology is a tool to be used* is not so much incorrect as it is incomplete. *Pencils, crayons and erasers* are also tools to be used. People that limit themselves to thinking in this manner are the real tools being used. They are the modern day sorcerer's apprentices.

This is a common criticism of technology, but a very important one that needs clarification. A software program is a collection of routines and programs that reside in hardware. The word "soft" refers to the quality or condition of being temporary or changeable. The word "hard" refers to the quality or condition of being consistent or unchangeable. The word "ware" refers to processes that are of the same general kind and used in a specific application. A computer is "hard" in the sense that its physical components are, allowing for some flexibility in changing or adding components, constant. A computer is "soft" in the sense that its electronic programs and routines are varied and changeable.

> **The future of e-Learning as a business is not in the provision of courseware systems, but in the provision of Mindware throughout all software.**

It is interesting to note a parallel in the training world. The term "hard skills" refers to the mastery of skill sets that are applied in a relatively consistent and stable environment. The hard-skinned technological environment provides the required sense of stability. For example, mastering the operation of a word processor—a software program—is a hard skill. The term "soft skills" refers to the mastery of skill sets that are applied in a relatively inconsistent and unstable environment. For example, leadership, conflict resolution, and time management are all soft. The soft-skinned human environment provides the required sense of instability.

Our ability to design, produce, and profit from the ways in which people can be used by software and hardware are extensive. It seems that there is an underlying plan to turn entire populations in the software's apprentice by "helping" them to be better operators. This is a generic characteristic of the training industry. We place an unreasonable amount of emphasis on training people with competencies that allow them to operate software as an end unto itself. The result is a massive group of trained people having computer skills that they are not entirely sure what to do with.

The word *training* has a wide range of use. A dog can be trained to sit. An infant can be toilet-trained. A school student is trained to obey a mechanical orientation to time. An athlete can be trained to run faster and jump higher. A soldier can be trained to follow order regardless of the surrounding danger. A plant can be trained to grow into a certain shape or direction. A weapon can be trained at a target. A train can carry people and supplies along a track. A train is also an orderly succession or series of thoughts or events; we can have a train of thoughts or refer to a train of events. A common factor across all of these descriptions is that training is a technique based on a clearly defined sequence of events in order to achieve a specific objective. Like software programming, a training curriculum is based on logical routines and sequential patterns with highly defined and specific outcomes.

Netg (www.netg.com) is currently one of the leading e-Training providers in United States and is a good example of how the Internet can make learning software more efficient. As of May 2001, their course catalogue available contains 1106 pages! The three courses available on Microsoft Word 2000 are divided into: a) basic user, b) proficient user and c) expert user. The notion of an *expert* is inappropriate and really means an *efficient* user. The courses are offered in different languages, but are not customized to various levels of literacy. It is projected by Netg that each of the three levels would take an average of six to eight hours, for a total of 18 to 24 hours. This is an important value proposition for potential clients, the development of "expertise" in the least amount of time possible. Microsoft Word 97 is "taught" in two levels in an average of 12 to 16 hours. Microsoft Word 95 is taught in 18 hours. "Learning" to use a browser such as Microsoft Internet Explorer 5 requires 6 to 8 hours of time.

The real value of training is to help people gain efficiency with software in the shortest amount of time possible. The learner, of course, needs to have some degree of facility with software before they can finds ways of applying it to a much higher and more important purpose. At the same time, these approaches incorrectly identify themselves as "e-Learning" when in fact they have very little to do with anything that can remotely be referred to as e-Learning. A more apt frame of reference for products such as Netg is "e-Training." The training virus has infected the world of digital technologies in epidemic proportions:

? How many times have we seen or experienced training dedicated to learning the functions of a word processor that is completely void of learning to become more skilled in the art of writing?

? How many times have we seen or experienced training dedicated to learning the functions of presentation software that is completely void of learning how to become more skilled in making a presentation?

? How many different on-line courses for software training does the world really need?

Filling the gap between efficient use of software and higher level application is the purpose of Mindware. Ultimately, the aim of Mindware is to provide the foundation for training itself.

The word Mindware comes from a different place. A mind is something we associate with thinking, intelligence, consciousness, emotion, spirit, perception, memory, and imagination. Our minds are more than a collection of routines and programs that direct our bodies. The human mind is inexorably connected with the human body in a psychobiological system of interaction; the mind does not merely direct the body nor does the body merely direct the mind. This is the intersection we refer to as the "mind-body connection." The word *ware* refers to its more archaic meaning of being aware, wary, watchful, or to beware of. In this sense, it is a quality of being alert, rather than a collection of similar processes and routines as in the word software.

Mindware: The specific alertness of mind required to develop critical and creative approaches for using software tools to facilitate learning.

Mindware immediately shifts our orientation away from the traditional training paradigm of people being apprentices to software to a new paradigm of people being the masters of software. The master is someone who teaches while at the same time remaining critically and creatively oriented to their own work. In e-Learning, technological tools *must* be placed in the service of human ingenuity. Mindware means that software is subservient and responsive to the people that are using it—it is a new way of thinking about *skills*.

To appreciate the idea of Mindware is also important in updating our understanding of the word *skill*. In general, a skill refers to a human proficiency, talent, or ability. It is interesting to note that the Middle English word *skil* was closely connected to the word *discernment*. To discern something means to perceive it with the senses or with the intellect in a distinct or different manner. This way of thinking about skill moves us into to the realm of criti-

168

cal and creative vitality. This means that the acquisition of skill with a word processor is inexorably linked to the improvement in the quality, not quantity, of one's written expression. In developing skill with a word processor, the ultimate aim is to qualitatively improve a person's written expression regardless of the writing style in question (e.g. fiction, nonfiction, technical, etc.). Mindware is a completely different context for teaching something as seemingly banal as word processing.

> *It is the "help" system already present in most software applications that has the greatest potential for building e-Learning that helps people through Mindware. The externalized help-training industry is already standing on quicksand. We will simply not need them in the long term.*

From a software training perspective, most programs come with well-designed help systems and Internet support tools for training. This is the proper home for home for training. We do not require the extensive numbers of "how to" books and services that needlessly proliferate in the industry. It would be far more effective to build alliances which serve to extend and enhance these existing "help" systems so that they can evolve more toward a real "e-Learning" systems. Microsoft Word already integrates: a) an on-line manual; b) an integrated and context-sensitive Help system in the software itself; and c) on-line help and tutoring from the Microsoft website. In its current form we would be hard pressed to refer to it as an e-Learning system, but it is clearly the most important basis for creating one. The application of Mindware to word processing results in some fundamental changes in our orientation to what "help" really means.

If a word processor is a tool to improve writing, then the techniques, methods, approaches, and strategies to improve the quality of writing should be completely integrated with the idea of "help." Mindware makes this a core demand and value proposition for helping people; we are not only helping people to become more efficient users of the software itself, we are also helping them to become more effective writers.

The easiest way to build a system of Mindware in a word processor would be to redesign the network of people involved in creating the *help* system itself. The designers and programmers of the word processing help system would form an alliance with professional writers from a diversity of fields. This new network alliance would focus on the question: "How can the existing help

FROM WORD PROCESSING TO THOUGHT PROCESSING

AIMS	TRAINING	MINDWARE
Coherence and clarity of writing	Software technique to create, manage and navigate a document using the document mapping tools.	*The use of document mapping to improve the organization, coherence and clarity of written expression.*
Editing and Revision	Software technique required to create, view and manage comments in a document.	*Integration of commenting with a constant process of editing and revision.*
Growth and Evolution of Written Expression	Software technique required to apply tracking changes to a document.	*The use of tracking changes to capture and review the various developmental stages of the writing process.*
Language Support	Software technique required to use spell check and grammar check tools.	*The real-time integration of literacy support strategies to improve vocabulary, comprehension and syntax.*

The aims for mindware training originate in the methods for improving the quality of writing as they can be reasonably supported by software tools.

The aims for software training originate in the requirements to master the software itself.

To transform software training into mindware training a clear understanding of how specific software tools can be used to support the broader and more comprehensive aim of improving written expression is required. Rather than learning all possible software functions, the learner is critically and creatively focused on how the software can be used to facilitate specific writing techniques that are cumbersome, difficult or impossible without it.

In the end, the effective use of word processing software has more to do with how written expression is improved rather than how easily the software can be manipulated to produce words.

system integrate strategies and tactics that lead to the qualitative improvement of writing?" The value proposition of the software is enormously improved not only in terms of the market punch but also in terms of the real value it gives to people.

Word processing provides a very familiar example. Mindware is, however, an idea that can be applied to *any* existing software application. The potential for the total transformation of other software applications such as operating systems, Internet browsers, communication tools, productivity tools, artistic tools, and so on is enormous. In many cases, the most effective tactical point for integrating Mindware is through the existing help systems already present. The end result of this strategy is the transparent pervasive integration of e-Learning support throughout all software. In order to achieve this, the fragmentation in the software industry between those that produce the actual software people use and those that produce secondary training software is eliminated. More importantly, our writing is concretely improved through our use of the word processor, our communications are improved through our use of communications tools, our operating systems evolve to personalized e-Learning systems, and so on.

> *The crisis of current practices in the software industry is the creation of a computer training market that is designed to teach efficiency in the absence of effectiveness.*

The basic requirement to achieve this is the creation of a new kind of network learning environment that supports new kinds of relationships. The participants in Mindware software development initiatives would include: a) designers; b) software programmers; c) learning architects; d) proven performers and experts (writers, financial planners, presenters, graphics artists, trainers, website producers, etc.) in their field, as well as an eclectic mix of people including journalists, criminal investigators, politicians, artists, educators, and so on. The creation of this new network learning environment is fundamental to the future evolution of all software production initiatives. The Interaction Design Matrix provides an organizational design and operational tool to support the environment.

A networked strategic initiative that embraces Mindware would immediately result in more valuable, desirable, sustainable, and durable product offerings. The software "upgrade" that constantly appears on the market is generally a variation on how to make the previous version easier and more stable. As such, they cannot really be presented as something which is truly innovative. The software sector has an important opportunity here to expand their already substantial market. By strategically changing their focus from such things as help systems, on-line support and FAQs, performance support systems, knowledge and data base archives, and traditional approaches to training and education toward a strategic direction that embraces Mindware they would immediately create a more valuable and desirable product offering. For example, this quite literally means that a company producing word processing software would be intensively engaged in marketing and selling software that is designed to qualitatively improve the written expression of the people using it. This is a very different proposition from the current emphasis on the use of templates that make the *appearance* of the document more pleasing.

Mindware positions *any* software application as a potential e-Learning environment. However, this e-Learning environment has little resemblance to those that are driven by learning management systems and courseware. The bottom line is that there are many more software functions in a single package than anyone needs to know; the mastery of specific software functions with the purpose of improving a human capability can lead to exponential improvements with respect to learning. Becoming efficient with a wide range of software routines doesn't mean I will learn or work more effectively.

What Is e-Learning Software?

When we think about e-Learning, we are reminded of specific kinds of software: course authoring tools, learning management systems, knowledge management systems, data mining systems, electronic performance support systems, and on-line courses. The corporate perspective on e-Learning, notably as a kind of electronic performance support system, is captured in Marc Rosenberg's *e-Learning: Strategies for Delivering Knowledge in the Digital Age* (Rosenberg, Marc 2001). The education perspective is uniformly concentrated on the development of on-line courses that include lectures, lessons, message boards, chat systems, video-conferencing tools, animation, and simulation, as well as assessment and tracking tools. This effort is exclusively aimed at extending the existing institutional practices to the Internet.

Both approaches are similar in kind in that they are designed to accelerate and distribute existing practices through the Internet. What is being accelerated and distributed (i.e. information and courses) remains largely unchanged. This kind of process is one that is emblematic of our tendency to retrieve past practices through new technologies, or as Marshall McLuhan said, "We tend to use the new to do the old."

Mindware acknowledges that these approaches to e-Learning have a place, but they are not in themselves comprehensive enough to understand the potential depth and breadth of e-Learning.

> *E-Learning software is not a monolithic platform or isolated event in the Cybersphere, it is a pervasive and distributed design perspective on how the entire range of Internet software tools can be used and integrated to support customized approaches to learning.*

Mindware is a strategic approach for transforming any Internet capable software into e-Learning software. Since the software industry does not currently embrace the idea of their products integrating e-Learning support in transparent and pervasive ways, the transformation of the software lies in the realm of how we choose to use it. Ideally, this problem will decline over time, but this does not imply that critical changes in our approach to using software cannot begin immediately. To achieve this, it is the users of the software who become the real designers. Their role cannot, obviously, be at the level of programming, but is more strategically centered in designing how the software is best used. This is the real domain for learning with respect to software tools.

In order to further answer the question "What is e-Learning software?" I have selected two common needs: a) improving writing through software; and b) improving reading through software. This is not to say that we should replace other methods of learning to read and write. We could easily apply similar processes to desktop management, Internet browsers, graphics design tools, and the like. However, beginning with the familiar is the easiest point of entry into the power of Mindware.

Network Writing and Reading

> *E-Learning software is any software that has the ability to reach into the Internet.*

From any desktop computer with Internet access, Microsoft Word can be used as e-Learning software. What allows this are certain kinds of software functions that are already available in the program:

THE WORD PROCESSOR AS E-LEARNING

AIMS · E-LEARNING

AIMS	E-LEARNING
The improvement of collaboration in writing.	1. **File - Send To**: Documents are distributed as email attachments.
The establishment of a community of practice for writing.	2. **Track Changes**: Multiple reviewers can edit documents and include their changes directly in the document. The changes made can be compared by the author and changes can be accepted or rejected.
Integration of resource and support.	3. **Commenting**: Multiple reviewers can tag parts of the document with comments. This, in effect, creates a kind of message board for the document itself.
The word processing document becomes an electronic portfolio in which the process of writing is transparent.	4. **Text Highlight**: Electronic highlighting can be used to direct attention to areas in question. 5. **Hypertext Links**: Connections to the Internet can be threaded throughout the document allowing for the transparent integration of language and resource support.
The extension of the word processing application through collaborative Internet tools.	6. **File - Versions**: A collection of versions can be saved that provide the developmental history of the document. 7. **Conferencing Support**: (e.g. MSN Messenger® and Microsoft NetMeeting®)

Readily available software applications can provide the basis for the creative development of an e-Learning platform at minimal cost.

The idea that e-Learning is equivalent to traditional on-line learning approaches (e.g. courseware) is too limiting. Any software application that has Internet functionality can be transformed by creative people into powerful e-Learning tools.

An author writes a book. From the author's point of view, the book represents a synthesis of his or her experiences up to that point in time. The book therefore has a cultural, emotional, and intellectual context. The book may refer to various points in history, various parts of the world, and various kinds of emotions. In doing so, the book on its own can be thought of as a network of relationships and associations that extend to fictional and non-fictional experiences expressed through text. Many copies of the book are published and sold. People read the text and comprehend it in a highly personal manner. The understanding that the author has of the book he or she wrote is not the same as the readership—there is no single understanding that is shared in totality. The common ground, or medium, is the unchanging text on the page, but a diversity of variations are improvised in the minds of the readers. We may read a review of the book in a newspaper, view an interview with the author on television, participate in a group discussion at the local coffee shop, or join an interest group on the WWW. The book's meaning beyond the text on the page is found in the network of relationships and associations it traverses. The book is not merely a singular entity but is in itself a network of interaction.

Ironically, the metamorphosis of the printed book into the e-book may offer a vibrant opportunity for e-Learning. Many software companies are failing to recognize the latent potential for e-Learning already present in their products.

In a seminar entitled "Beyond the Book: Publishing Redefined" Adobe Systems Inc. revealed its vision of the future of publishing. The purpose of the presentation was to address the transformation of the publishing industry from the traditional book publishing model to the new work flow requirements of *network publishing*. The core of the idea is a rich concept of *network publishing*, or the idea of creating content once but be able to effortlessly publish it in many ways. It is basically a revised workflow process for a publisher that results in the immediate dissemination of products to print, print-on-demand, e-Books, PDAs and the WWW. The core software to develop this content is Adobe's Framemaker+SGML 6.0. The gateway to networked publishing for the audience on the World Wide Web is Adobe Acrobat e-Book Reader 2.1. Through this software the user can download purchase, view, and create a personal library of digital books. The e-commerce and e-business models are driven through the Adobe Content Server web application, which has a focus on the management of transactions between consumer and supplier with an emphasis on the protection of intellectual property rights. Authors can self-publish through services such as iUniverse (www.iuniverse.com). (See *Network Publishing* at www.adobe.com.) Forester Research has projected that the emerging e-Book industry will approach

$7.8 billion USD by 2005, and that 42% of that industry will be in electronic textbook market. E-Learning was not a topic or an area identified as being important, however, it is without question the most important opportunity of the product.

By applying the principles of Mindware we can reveal some latent potential for e-Learning in e-Books:

THE E-BOOK AS E-LEARNING

AIMS	E-LEARNING
Reader maps relationships within book.	**1. Bookmarks:** The reader develops a system of bookmarks to identify relevant connections across the span of the e-Book.
Reader maps relationships from the e-Book to the Internet.	**2. Internet Links:** The reader develops a system of bookmarks to the Internet that provide additional enhancements and resources on top of the author's text.
Reader integrates their own comments on top of the author's text for electronic collaboration.	**3. Commenting:** The reader tracks his or her own insight and ideas throughout the reading process. These comments may be shared electronically with other readers in a community of practice.
Reader transforms key words into hypertext linkages.	**4. Customization of the Author's Text:** The reader is given a range of possibilities to alter and modify the author's original text.
Customized language support services.	**5. Literacy Support:** The reader develops customized vocabulary lists, stylistic examples, etc., specific to that e-Book. These lists can be shared and collaborated upon electronically.

The benefit of e-Books will be discovered in their potential for the provision of e-Learning. It is unlikely they will find a home in reading for personal enjoyment.

The flexibility of e-Books make heavy cognitive demands on the reader and are best thought of as an e-Learning habitat. The integration of software functionality to extend and enhance the reading process provide opportunities for more intense and concentrated forms of reading, as well as literacy support.

The convergence of network publishing, e-Learning, and education is an important one. The publisher's role will become increasingly more influenced by designing books as a learning experience and the educator's role will become increasingly more influenced by their own empowerment to publish. In fact, the very survival of the publisher may be dependent upon their ability to change their identity and the roles that they play in a world where every individual can self-publish with or without the aid of a traditional publisher. Educators will increasingly require the publisher to be an intellectual advisor, process consultant, and technology solutions provider.

Through Mindware, the acts of writing and reading become inseparable from e-Learning. They originate in network learning environments, they are empowered by human ingenuity, and they are guided by lifework. There is no separation between them, only connections.

At the center of the writing and reading examples is the unavoidable reality that our writing and reading processes are no longer solitary and isolated enterprises, but a network learning environment to be explored and re-explored over time.

The Mindware Industry

There is an increasing tendency to equate the acquisition of broadband networks with the purchase of expensive on-line course delivery and performance support systems. This is equivalent to equating the acquisition of gold-plated pencils and the purchase of expensive paper with improvements in education. A great deal of financial investment, time, and energy has been and will continue to be needlessly wasted on the pursuit of the holy grail of the *killer app* in e-Learning—there simply isn't one and more importantly, we don't need one. Further, streaming video and audio through broadband networks is not unlike watching television and listening to the radio. The current advantages of streaming technologies are modest.

The creation of a Mindware Industry is the next evolution of the software industry.

A Mindware Industry is a network learning environment of designers, programmers, and end users that focus on promoting effective uses of software. E-Learning as a software industry dedicated to the design and production of training materials and on-line courses is, thankfully, an endangered species.

The value of Mindware for learning institutions is substantial:

⇒ **Inexpensive**
There are no financial requirements beyond a basic network infrastructure and the availability of the word processing software itself.

⇒ **Customizable**
Can be developed for any age group and accommodate any purpose for writing.

⇒ **Focused**
The training program can focus specifically on the kinds of skills people need to have in order to support the e-Learning dimension without leaving the software itself.

⇒ **Install Base**
Word processing software is one of the most commonly available applications used to support learning.

⇒ **Extendable**
The e-Learning dimension can be extended through other readily available tools that promote real-time interaction (e.g. chat, video conferencing) as well as document linkages to the Internet (i.e. sources of information, reference support, projects and events).

The disadvantages reside in the level of tactics and implementation and do not detract from the need to institute Mindware as a comprehensive approach to the use of software.

Mindware may not be an approach that is welcomed by many business leaders in the e-Learning industry. First, there is dramatically less need for the products they are selling. Second, the new approach creates a value proposition far beyond the value of their own current offering. Third, the systemic deployment of Mindware throughout the software production and training process is sustainable, durable, and fundamentally innovative. Fourth, the questionable focus many institutions of learning place on improving their network infrastructure would normalize itself by redistributing more funds to the training and deployment of Mindware. Fifth, the consumer demands placed on what constitutes "value" in a software upgrade is far more sophisticated and demanding. Sixth, the illusion of the *killer app* in e-Learning is

E-LEARNING: STRATEGIC DIRECTIONS

1

Leverage Existing Software Penetration
Common and widely distributed software packages have a great deal of latent potential for the support of e-Learning. The examples above of networked writing and networked reading represent a brief sampling of the total range of possibilities. The software to support a wide dispersion of e-Learning is already available on most computers.

2

Elevate Operating System Functionality to Support e-Learning
The customization and personalization of the computer desktop is the primary consideration for the development of e-Learning software. The current emphasis on trite customization through images and sounds will be evolved through the increasing provision of Mindware.

3

Elevate Web Browser Functionality to Support e-Learning
The web browser is a critical software tool for e-Learning. The transparent integration of tools to support network learning environments, exploration and lifework can transform the browser from a tool for observation into a tool for learning. Many of the elements already exist, but are not guided or coordinated by a meaningful approach to learning.

4

Elevate "Help" Systems to e-Learning Systems
The help system in many software applications are already moving toward the provision of e-Learning resources. The result will be the eventual elimination of the need for e-Learning companies to provide on-line software training resources.

5

The Collaborative Toolbox
Elevate current chat, message board and conferencing technologies to collaborative support for e-Learning. Structure the use of these tools against the Interaction Design Matrix.

6

Redirect Budgetary Resources
What is missing from the e-Learning equation is intellectual opportunity not technological opportunity. There is no real need to deplete financial resources in order to acquire centralized and expensive ASP services, learning management systems, and broadband network infrastructures. Financial resources need to be redirected to professional development in order to make use of technological resources that are inexpensive and readily available.

killed. Seventh, a new organizational infrastructure and design process based on network learning environments would need to be integrated into the corporate organizational chart. Eighth, the kind of intelligence required by the e-Learning software producer becomes dramatically more demanding and complex.

Strategic Directions: Mindware

ELIMINATE MONOLITHIC E-LEARNING SOFTWARE PLATFORMS

The killer application, the best courseware development tool, the ideal learning management system, the development of reusable learning objects, the perfection of on-line assessment tools, and the like have little to do with the future of e-Learning.

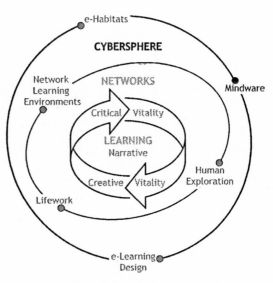

ELIMINATE THE TRAINING OF SOFTWARE AS AN END UNTO ITSELF

There is no further need to continue to develop more and more training programs and tools to teach people how to use software. We have more than enough already and many of the "help" systems within existing software applications are already beginning to make this need redundant.

PROMOTE THE PERVASIVE INTEGRATION OF MINDWARE IN ALL SOFTWARE

All software has potential to support e-Learning. The design focus for the next wave of e-Learning will be completely centered on the effective use of technology to support more comprehensive and sophisticated goals for learning.

DRAMATICALLY INCREASE CONSUMER DEMANDS AND EXPECTATIONS ON SOFTWARE PRODUCERS

Consumers must expect and demand that all support for learning how to use the software be completely integrated with the software itself. There should be little need for other companies to produce secondary support materials such as "How To" books and CD-ROMs. The fact that these materials exist only serves to indicate a lack of ability on the part of the producer to increase the value of their product on their own.

COLLECT AND DISSEMINATE EXEMPLARY NARRATIVES OF MINDWARE

The provision of narratives captures and elevates the creative and unusual uses of software by people. These narratives have everything to do with the discovery of unique applications of software, and little to do with the "How To" aspects of the software.

9. E-LEARNING DESIGN

The future of e-Learning technology requires a network learning environment that integrates the corporate, governmental, educational, and cultural sectors. The rationale for this is based on: a) no one sector has the necessary intelligence to evolve e-Learning to new levels of value and performance; b) learning is a source of design that transcends any one sector; and c) network technologies are most effectively developed

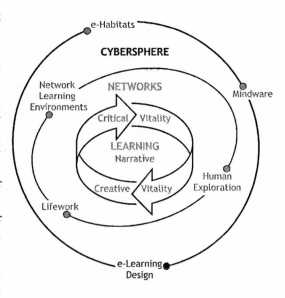

by powerful, adaptive, and flexible networks of relationships.

What are the design requirements that lead directly to new and innovative practices in e-Learning?

In the end, the e-Learning design results in a unified and distributed array of network tools that are combined and repurposed in response to the needs of the learner.

Chapter Design

The e-Learning Intelligence Network
The learning experiences required for e-Learning designers are fundamentally different from current practices in the training of web architects, interface designers, and programmers.

Lifelong and Lifewide e-Learning
The Experience Designer model as a foundation for e-Learning design.

The e-Learning Intelligence Network

The traditional approach to e-Learning design in the technology sector is based on a variation of the traditional industrial-age production model. While the roles within this model have been changed in order to accommodate new kinds of expertise and skills, the overall process remains quite similar to an assembly line. Some of the new media industry role descriptions include the new media producer, information architect, interface designer, software engineer, software programmer, graphics designer, sound designer, video producer, knowledge manager, database architect, usability expert, content producer, trainers, chief learning officer, and of course the mercurial and ever-illusive realm of the new media consultant. These new roles and functions, however, still function within a traditional organizational design and operating structure. At the same time, the expertise required to make e-Learning software in the first place is clearly centered in this sector.

The traditional approach to e-Learning design in the educational sector is based on a traditional education production model. The existing administrative bureaucracy serves as the basis for improving efficiency through the use of administrative support technologies. The existing approaches to curriculum and instruction serve as the basis for extending traditional practices through e-Learning. Software commonly referred to as "course authoring" software is the symbol for maintaining traditional practice. Since the departmental structures within our schools, colleges, and universities remain mired in departmental protectionism and inflexible role descriptions, a substantial roadblock for developing effective e-Learning practices is built. Most innovation occurs in the underground of the *skunk-works*. At the same time, the innovative educators that understand learning, education, and training better than most are centered in this sector.

The approach to e-Learning design in the government sector is harder to find. For the most part, these initiatives are myopically focused on issues of technological access and information dissemination. Even government-sponsored initiatives such as SchoolNet, while providing a useful communications structure for linking people in schools, remain mired in replicating traditional practices on the Internet. There is a complete lack of a coordinated and strategic policy for the national development of e-Learning. Without a national policy for e-Learning, the future development of the Internet will be dramatically impaired. The only means to balance the dominant trend of the commercialization of the World Wide Web is to counter it with an equally dominant trend to promote learning. The people understanding the most urgent needs of the public and private sectors are centered in this sector.

The cultural sector, perhaps the greatest symbol of tradition itself, also finds itself in the same conundrum. Many of the Cybersphere initiatives in the cultural sector are aimed at such things as digital museums, cross-cultural events on the Internet, digital archiving of tradition, and on-line libraries. In other words, they seem to have intensified a "see but don't touch" approach. At the same time, there are many highly innovative initiatives by the artistic community at large. This community of cultural pioneers and artistic entrepreneurs is a vibrant source of how creativity can be applied to the Cybersphere. The people that can truly "think out of the box" are a strong force in this sector.

> *We have embraced an age of "doing the same old thing anywhere, anytime, and in any amount."*

It is somewhat enigmatic that we refer to ideals such as "meeting the needs of the learner," "individualized learning," and "customized learning," while at the same time developing and implementing tools into which the learner has no input nor any real ability to customize or individualize. The reason for this is that current e-Learning systems are largely closed. The kind of individualization we experience inside of these experiences is highly controlled: a) the information we are supposed to learn is largely pre-determined; b) the advantage of accessing e-Learning anytime, anywhere is limited to accessing the same thing anytime, anywhere; c) the "interactivity" available in these environments is either of the "point and click" type, or contribution to message boards and chat systems; d) the assessment and evaluation procedures dominating e-Learning are digital versions of antiquated testing procedures; and e) the software platform includes "customization" tools that are limited in scope and do not generally affect the character of the learning environment itself. In other words, individualized and customized learning thrives inside of the limitations and control structures defined by the design of the software.

The polar opposites of the five criticisms above are also problematic. It would be incorrect to leap to conclusions that: a) information architecture is not important; b) the idea of accessing e-Learning anytime and anywhere is not of value; c) interactivity is a hit-or-miss proposition; d) assessment and evaluation are not important; and e) software cannot be designed to promote higher levels of individualization and customization. In fact, *Part One: Learning* and *Part Two: Networks* have clearly shown that these ideas are critical and fundamental. It is not the idea that is the problem, it is the implementation of it.

A designer of e-Learning is literally anyone that makes use of e-Learning. The idea of an e-Learning Designer as being a specialized area of expertise that is focused on information architecture, interface design, content production, assessment and tracking tools, etc., is ineffective. Regardless of who creates the information, the unavoidable reality is that the *meaning* is created on the other end. Regardless of who creates the interface design, it is the user's interface with their own experience that is of primary importance in learning. Regardless of who creates the content for e-Learning, the understanding of it is always created on the other end. Regardless of who creates the assessment and tracking mechanisms, it is the users on the other end who make the ultimate decision about how to apply knowledge in their lives. E-Learning production methodologies that ignore these glaringly obvious realities will at best celebrate fleeting moments of success. The people who are asked to use the e-Learning system are ultimately far more powerful and decisive than those responsible for producing it.

> *We are all designers of e-Learning; no one can be excluded from this experience. E-Learning is unique and not similar in kind to e-Business or e-Commerce. E-Learning must rise above the traditional customer-vendor relationship.*

The first way to create some equilibrium here is to clarify and expose the language we use to promote and market e-Learning systems and consulting. Often, the corporate and consultant response is adept at developing a kind of language to respond to the known challenges and criticisms of potential clients. The notion of a *needs analysis* provides an example of this. The proposition is that a corporation or consultant will conduct a "needs analysis" in order to ensure that the requirements for successful implementation with the client are met. Typically, recommendations are made about supplying a "needed" kind of content and a "needed" set of web tools. The host corporation or consultant will then broker the best kinds of content and web development relationships to meet the proposed needs and thereby make the sale. Herein lies the holy grail of the value proposition, or the means for a corporation or consultant to create revenue streams—or, more fundamentally, to justify their existence. Whether or not the product provided was actually needed or not is a different question.

This kind of process may be more effective in the realm of technology integration when clients do not have the inside knowledge. The installation and maintenance of computer technology, however, is a vastly different proposition than the "installation" of e-Learning. The "inside knowledge" about e-Learning is always immersed inside and pervasive throughout the host organization. The traditional form of an externalized "needs analysis" is largely irrelevant with respect to learning. In fact, e-Learning itself is the most ongoing and durable form of needs analysis in itself. While externally produced solutions to needs may have a degree of utility, ultimately the needs of an organization or individual originate internally. The input into the design and on-going adaptation of e-Learning is widely distributed responsibility. The traditional vendor-consumer relationship is an ineffective structure for the future development of e-Learning. This is not to say that these kinds of traditional relationships will not persist in e-Learning projects, but it is to say that they are not likely to add any value to the evolution of e-Learning as a powerful unifying force on the Internet. (See table "The e-Learning Intelligence Network" on the following page.)

The idea of *The E-Learning Intelligence Network* is a means to set the stage for the elevation of e-Learning as a powerful force of change throughout the Internet. It is decidedly not a committee and special task force, but a living and vibrant *network learning environment*. The environment is empowered by the exploration of human ingenuity as it is applied to issue of the future of e-Learning.

THE E-LEARNING INTELLIGENCE NETWORK

THE CONTRIBUTORS ⟷ THE LEARNERS

1

The Government Sector
Educational policy-makers will elevate their thinking from issues of Internet access and information architecture to a more critical consideration of learning, its relationship to networks and a strategic implementation of e-Learning.

Ministers, economic development, health and welfare specialists, patients, homeless people, emergency service personnel, military strategists, intelligence experts, law enforcement personnel, etc.

2

The Education/Training Sector
Educators will focus on promoting human ingenuity through e-Learning. The retrieval of the traditional course and program of study paradigm will gradually become less dominant.

Students, parents, teachers, professors, administrators, curriculum designers, instructional designers, corporate trainers and consultants, publishers, research centers, etc.

3

The Corporate Sector
Companies that fail to evolve away from the production of software training programs, courseware authoring tools and learning management systems will become extinct. The future of the e-Learning industry lies in the elevation of current practices to a more stable foundation.

CEO, executive managers, human resource specialists, sales specialists, marketing specialists, advertising and public relations specialists, financial specialists, administrative and support staff, etc.

4

The Cultural Sector
Cultural institutions will embrace learning, networks and the cybersphere as an important source of cultural development and design. Institutions will increasingly become part of an expanding network of centers for cultural innovation.

Journalists, movie producers, librarians, museum curators, theatre directors, actors and actresses, musicians, artists, athletes halls, sports, movie-goers, shoppers, etc.

For e-Learning to evolve, the development of mechanisms to share and integrate the efforts of these four sectors of society is critical.

Unified Design

Lifelong and Lifewide e-Learning

Strategically, e-Learning is a system that needs to be centered in both a life-long and lifewide electronically networked domain. The experience designer embraces this orientation to e-Learning within a more comprehensive and guiding framework for total experience of learning.

LIFELONG E-LEARNING

Learning

Narrative and Modern Life: Capture, archive and disseminate exemplary narratives in order to create a library of experience. Enhance each story with information as a means to enhance and extend its meaning.

Critical Vitality: Question and clarify the underlying assumptions and purpose of exemplary narratives. Identify the strengths and weaknesses of the narrative in relation to local situations and circumstances.

Creative Vitality: Create, invent, design, build and implement unique patterns of thought that are distributed throughout the repertoire of narratives. Develop an action plan for using these patterns in society.

Networks

Network Learning Environments: Establish adaptive learning environments that integrate a wide variety of people, places and things across authentic, cybersphere, electronic and print experiences.

The Explorers: Engage learners in capturing, archiving case studies and applying processes of exploration that originate in the lives of exemplary people in the world.

Lifework: Capture, archive and develop principles from people's experiences in finding employment, a career and their lifework. Shape and guide the explorations into a comprehensive and personal plan for lifework.

Cybersphere

e-Learning Habitats: Survey, analyze and test a wide range of potential e-Learning habitats and tools. Identify enhancements and improvements in their use to better support learning.

Mindware: Approach *all* software as an e-Learning tool. Develop methods for using the software that results in effective use as a learning tool.

e-Learning Design: Synthesize the design process of e-Learning with *The Experience Designer* model in order to work toward a global and unified system of e-Learning throughout the Internet.

Strategic Directions: e-Learning Design

BUILD A COMPREHENSIVE E-LEARNING INTELLIGENCE NETWORK

The future of e-Learning is dependent upon providing unity, not uniformity, across the diversity of possibilities for leveraging the cybersphere to support a holistic approach to learning.

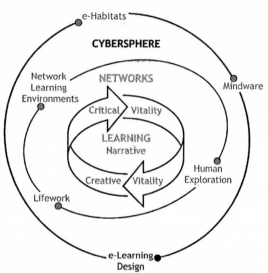

DISTRIBUTE THE RESPONSIBILITY FOR DESIGN TO ALL

The future of the Internet will be intimately connected to our ability to create greater diversity in design methods and production processes. E-Learning is the most important consideration for inventing the future of the Internet. The designers and producers of the next generation of e-Learning will have a more sophisticated and complex set of abilities than we see in current practice.

PROMOTE EXPERIENCE DESIGN AS A FRAMEWORK FOR E-LEARNING DESIGN

The design of e-Learning as an experience is a more profitable design perspective than the design of e-Learning as an interface. In this sense, the "interface" is learning, and not merely screen, speakers, and mouse.

INCREASE LEARNER NEED FOR RESPONSIBILITY AND ACCOUNTABILITY

Personalization in e-Learning allows the learner to select, modify, and discover new uses of the software tools provided. It is not merely a matter of applying preferred colors, graphics skins, and so on. Personalization is the means to invite the learner into design as collaboration.

COLLECT AND DISSEMINATE EXEMPLARY NARRATIVES OF E-LEARNING DESIGN

The provision of narratives captures and elevates creative and unusual design practices in the software industry. The goal of the e-Learning designer is to contribute to the creation of a unified, global, and democratic distribution of e-Learning opportunities.

EPILOGUE: ENDURING FREEDOM

Our clear and present hope is that freedom must be enduring and that we must learn to endure the consequences of freedom. This is the spirit, hope, and responsibility of Enduring Freedom.

My heart and spirit is with the victims, families of the victims and survivors of the September 11, 2001 holocaust. My respect and admiration is with all those who faced the consequences with unselfish heroism. Our hope for the future clearly rests in the present day and future heros that will unavoidably emerge from the dark circumstances in humankind.

It is now late October, 2001. I find it very difficult to summon the concentration required to finish this book. I continually ask myself, "What is the value of learning in the face of evil?" It is a question and exploration that will remain with me for the rest of my life, for I cannot imagine pursuing life in anyway *hopeful* without it. Another question—"How does a person such as myself who, at least for the moment, is distanced from the authentic experience of terrorism find a voice to talk about it?" Again, a question that will not be resolved here. We are standing at the dawn of a completely new age of questions.

The heroism in the face of the criminal insanity that marked September 11 has been overwhelming. There are narratives that have and will continue to emerge as profound and fundamental sources of design for learning. I do not wish to sound detached or clinical by framing these horrible events as a "learning opportunity," but it is without any question the most profound learning opportunity that we will be presented with in our lives. Learning never occurs in the absence of emotion. None of us, wherever we may live, should be under any illusion that "evil can't happen to us." More importantly, none of us should be held captive by an unnecessary pathology of fear.

Terrorism is thus violence—or, equally important, the threat of violence—used and directed in pursuit of, or in service of, a political act. . . . it is a planned, calculated, and indeed systemic act. . . . Terrorism is designed to create power where there is none or to consolidate power where there is very little. [Hoffman, 1998 #95]

The above definition is important. The tool of terrorism is violence, whether it is acted out or not. The intended effect of violence is fear. The intended result of this fear is political power. It is also important to note what is *not* in this definition—religion, spirituality, dignity, integrity, and a basic respect for human life are not in any way related to the definition of terrorism. They may, however, be used as tools of propaganda, or more appropriately, tools for lying. I would add to this definition that terrorism is a "planned, calculated, and indeed systemic act" of lying, deception, and deprivation. There is *no* truth to be found in the terrorist—they quite literally live in a completely delusional state.

Let me share my own assumptions in these confusing times before describing what this means to experience design:

1. Good and Evil
The act of defending an enduring freedom for all is *right*. Any act of terrorism is *wrong*. There are no shades of grey, no basis for finding a middle ground, and no debate. We are staring directly into the abyss of the eternal struggle between *good* and *evil* in which we are *right* and they are *wrong*. Terrorist organizations are nothing less than the incarnation of *evil*. Of course, they describe us in exactly the same terms.

2. The Network of the Human Spirit
There is an emerging network that transcends the political and the economic. We know that politics and economics always play a part, but this emergence, which I will call the *network of the human spirit,* is transcendent. This network *must* be a core source of design for *any* education system.

3. The Hero's Journey
The most important source of inspiration for all of us are the heroic acts of the people who are, unfortunately, authentically experiencing this tragedy. I maintain that the lives of these people and their narratives in the face of this awful confluence in modern life are a far more profound "curriculum" for learning than anything a traditional subject discipline or expert could ever hope to "teach."

4. The Profound Power of Learning
It is unfortunately clear that the critical and creative vitality of humankind is as much present in good as it is in evil. The terrorist perspective is fundamentally evil and therefore wrong in our world, but that is not to say that these misguided people are not capable of critical and creative thought. The humanist and democratic perspective is fundamen-

tally good and therefore right in our world, it is at least equally capable of critical and creative thought. The survivor of this new campaign will primarily be the one who is superior at *learning*. We are very clearly seeing the unacceptable degree to which we have come to rely on technology and how it has limited our ability to learn.

5. *The Abuse of Religion*
To make any connection at all between a viable religious perspective and the events of September 11 is a grave mistake. To say that some terrorists continually abuse religion in order to create a false justification for their acts of violence is correct. To react to terrorism with a gross over-generalization about a particular faith and seek revenge against an entire religious system is also evil, and constitutes a terrorist act in itself.

Network learning environments are now a media event. We are beginning to see fleeting glimpses into terrorist networks, terrorist cells, and terrorist training camps. *Training* is a very appropriate word, for it is a kind of training akin to training animals to perform in a circus. The terrorist training camp is in fact a kind of network learning environment—a repertoire of specific kinds of interaction and exploration that are designed to have a very specific effect. Inside these training camps we see children as young as nine and ten years old receiving training. Eliminating the clear and present danger of terrorism through the military is of course a primary and justified response, but until we are able to change the character of the terrorist learning environment we will not be able to eliminate terrorism. There are those that say that terrorism cannot be completely eliminated from our world. Where they get this knowledge from is a complete mystery, but to condemn humanity to the eternal presence of terrorism is wrong. Terrorism is *not* a universal absolute and it can be *completely* eradicated. This will ultimately occur through the power of learning, not through the initial and necessary military response. This *learning* must be global and unified in scope.

We are also beginning to see completely new patterns of interactivity emerge through coalitions and the creation of "departments" designed to integrate and synthesize communications and intelligence across separate elements (e.g. The Office of Homeland Security as a means to synthesize the intelligence of more than forty federal agencies). It is unfortunate and unnecessary to wait until a tragedy occurs before developing network learning environments. Attorney General John Ashcroft brilliantly stated in a press conference that "We are all learning as we go." This is a statement of profound strength and character. We, as a society of learners, can no longer limit ourselves to the bureaucratic pathology of compartments, isolated areas of expertise, and irrelevant assessment practices. Networks of learners are the solution, not only as a response to tragedy, but for every person of any age. The new leadership, the new strategists, and the new intelligence experts will all be unified through network learning environments, for there is *no* leadership, strategy, or intelligence without a network. Moreover, there is no learning of value without a network.

There is a very real need to protect ourselves from excessive yet understandable forms of pathology. At the same time, we will all to varying degrees be placed squarely in the line of sights of fear, anxiety, stress, desperation, insecurity, and depression. This is unavoidable. These kinds of emotional viruses are both a reason for fear *and more importantly a reason for hope*. We must ensure that if we err, we err on the side of hope. This leads me repeat (see *Chapter 1. Narrative and Modern Life*) one of the most important sources of inspiration for experience design:

> **It's important to live life with the experience, and therefore the knowledge, of its mystery and your own mystery. This gives life new radiance, a new harmony, a new splendor. Thinking in mythological terms helps to put you in accord with the inevitable of this vale of tears. You learn to recognize the positive values in what appear to be the negative moments and aspects of your life. The big question is whether you are going to be able to say a hearty yes to your adventure. (Campbell, Joseph 1988)**

We are all faced with a new and horrific *mystery* and are immersed in an *inevitable vale of tears*. It is the duty and responsibility of education to determine how everyone can be helped "to say a hearty yes to [their] adventure." Aiming an education system or program at anything less than this denigrates the human experience. In response to the tragic fallout from September 11, there are signs of this courage and strength in various education systems. Many students are involved in volunteerism in support of the families of the victims as well as emergency service workers. Many websites are emerging designed to build support. Many sensitive and responsible teachers are helping students to find a sense of stability and identity in what they observe. This is a very clear symbol of the power of the human spirit and the emergence of a narrative for living.

Epilogue: Enduring Freedom

One of the most profound "Central Intelligence Agencies" we can aspire to create is through the metamorphosis of the education system from an information agency to an intelligence network.

As an institutional system and organizational structure, however, the education system remains blinded by its own mechanics. Here I refer not to the people in the system, but the bureaucratized forms of curriculum, instruction, and assessment that drive it. There is no opportunity to assume an adventure in a system that is unresponsive to change. In my own local experience, I have found that while helpful discussions have taken place with students and helpful letters have been sent to parents, the actual experience of schooling has not changed in response to September 11. I know of one concrete example in which a student in a high school has spent a total of ten minutes in a discussion about the events of September 11—it is now late October. Worse, history is the same history, science is the same science, math is the same math, geography is the same geography, and the standardized tests that are falsely promoted as a means to prepare us for society continue to flow. So let it be written, so let it be done.

Of course, it is far too much to expect a sudden adaptation or transformation of education in such a short period of time. But there should be an expectation of adaptation. The reason for this is that there is no mechanism in either the bureaucratic structure, curriculum design, instructional methodologies, or assessment techniques to rapidly respond to the events taking place in the world. Helpful discussions, letters, and volunteerism aside, the only way to interpret this is that the organizational design of education as a system cannot respond effectively. At the same time, we live in a world in which rapid and thoughtful response is critical. If terrorism is a battle to be faced by millions over a long period of time, then being adaptive, responsive, and strategic is fundamental.

If this horrific act of terrorism is not an inspiration to change our education systems, then it is hard to imagine what will ever inspire them to change. The symbol of the new education system is the hope, tragedy, narratives, myths, people, and meaning that are embraced in the pursuit of the ideal of enduring freedom.

Further compounding this problem is that the minds, hearts, and hands of administrators, teachers, students, and parents are denigrated by the primacy of information. The black hole between what is really happening in the world and the continual drone of the same old information in education systems is dramatic. A counter to this criticism might be to say that it is important to maintain consistency and stability in order to pursue our lives as normally as possible in these difficult times. There are many problems with this line of thought: a) Whose definition of normal is this and why should I believe it really matters? b) Is this version of consistency and stability really a means to hide from our own inadequacies and fears of facing reality? c) Do we help people deal with fear by helping them to accept and travel through it, or do we help them by touching the surface of these fears and hoping that they find a way? We stand in the face of an educational challenge that is lifelong and lifewide in proportion.

Corporations face a similar struggle for enduring freedom. This is not only a matter of economic recovery. It may be time to stop and look and the products and services we aspire to create at a systemic level. We can do this by firmly placing those material things we seek in life firmly against the images of September 11. Since our economy, for the most part, is devoid of human narratives of heroism, there is now a real foundation for the things we do in it. The brilliant, famous, and wealthy CEO who rescues a company from certain financial disaster or designs the latest merger is a very insignificant figure when placed side-by-side with a single individual on ground zero. I wonder how many people still covet the newest versions of software, and if they do, what are their reasons? It is not that our lives should not have some dimension of material pursuit, but perhaps it is time to look at exactly how much of our time and resources go into the production of things for their own sake and what their real value is in the larger reality of the world.

The design of our private and public experiences has changed in ways we are only beginning to comprehend. The symbol of *Enduring Freedom* is a powerful opportunity and critical source of design for learning in our present time.

> *From the pain come the dream*
> *From the dream come the vision*
> *From the vision come the people*
> *From the people come the power*
> *From this power come the change*
>
> *(Peter Gabriel)*

196

References

1. Biko, S. (1978). The Testimony of Steve Biko: His beliefs about Black Consciousness, in his own words recorded at a political trial. Great Britain, Maurice Temple Smith Ltd.

2. Brin, D. (1998). Transparent Society: Will Technology Force Us To Choose Between Privacy and Freedom? Reading, Massachusetts, Persus Books.

3. Brody, R. Virus of the Mind.

4. Burke, J. (1996). The Pinball Effect.

5. Campbell, J. (1988). The Power of Myth. New York, Doubleday.

6. Cervantes, M. d. (1993). Don Quixote. Great Britain, Wordsworth Editions Limited.

7. Cronenberg, D. (1982). Videodrome. D. Cronenberg.

8. Cruikshank, B. (2001). Billions Have No Need, Interest, or PCs for Web, Reuters Limited: 2.

9. Dewey, J. (1938). Experience and Education. New York, Collier Books.

10. Diamond, S. (1996). Anger, Madness and the Daimonic: The Psychological Genesis of Violence, Evil, and Creativity. New York, State University of New York Press.

11. Dickens, C. (1854). Hard Times. England, Penguin Books Ltd.

12. DiManno, R. (2001). "A Teacher with Reason and Passion." The Toronto Star. Toronto.

13. Emerson, R. W. (1841). Self-Reliance.

14. EQAO (2000). Ontario Provincial Report on Achievement, 1999-2000. Toronto, Educational Quality and Accountability Office.

15. Freire, P. (1970). Pedagogy of the Oppressed. New York, Herder and Herder.

16. Gabriel, P. (1993). Xplora.

17. Gardner, H. (2000). The Disciplined Mind: Beyond Facts and Standardized Tests, The K-12 Education That Every Child Deserves. New York, Penguin Group.

18. Heim, M. (1993). The Metaphysics of Virtual Reality. New York, Oxford University Press, Inc.

19. Huxley, A. (1962). Island. New York, Harper and Row, Publishers.

20. Innis, H. (1951). The Bias of Communication. Toronto, University of Toronto Press.

21. Issacs, W. (1999). Dialogue and the Art of Thinking Together. New York, Doubleday.

22. Kantrowitz, B. (2001). "A Year in the Life." Newsweek.

23. Kondro, W. (2001). "Canada In Creativity Crisis." National Post. Toronto.

24. Marion, C. (1998). "What Is the EPSS Movement and What Does It Mean to Information Designers?" News and Views.

25. McAdams, D. (1993). The Stories We Live By: Personal Myths and the Making of the Self. New York, The Guilford Press.

26. McLuhan, M. (1969). Interview. Playboy.

27. McLuhan, M. a. Q. F. (1967). The Medium Is the Message: An Inventory of Effects. Toronto, Bantam Books.

28. OECD (2001). Investing in Competencies for All. Paris, Organization for Economic Co-operation and Development.

29. Pearson, P. (2001). "Creativity Crisis? Canada Rocks." National Post. Toronto.

30. Post, N. (2001). "Mental Health Affects the Bottom Line." National Post. Toronto.

31. Postman, N. (1995). The End of Education: Redefining the Value of School. New York, Alfred A. Knopf.

32. Project, T. D. H. (1997). Institution for Building the Soul: From An Interview With John Van Cleve.

33. Rosenberg, M. (2001). e-Learning: Strategies for Delivering Knowledge in the Digital Age. New York, McGraw-Hill.

34. Russell, B. (1928). "Machines and Emotions." Skeptical Essays.

35. Sennett, R. (1999). The Corrosion of Character: The Personal Consequences of Work in the New Capitalism. New York, W. W. Norton and Company, Inc.

36. Star, T. (2001). "World Indifferent to Hunger: U.N." Toronto Star. Toronto.

37. Sternberg, R. E. (2000). Handbook of Intelligence. Cambridge, Cambridge University Press.

38. TechKnowLogia (2001). International Journal of Technologies for the Advancement of Knowledge and Learning, Knowledge Enterprise, Inc.

39. UN (1948). Universal Declaration of Human Rights, United Nations General Assembly.

40. Weihenmayer, E. (2001). Touch The Top Of The World: A Blind Man's Journey To Climb Farther Than The Eye Can See. New York, Penguin Putnam Inc.

41. Wright, J. (2000). Ontario Children and Youth Mental Health. Toronto, IPSOS-Reid: 2.

About the Author

Brian Alger has been exploring the connections between learning and new technologies in many parts of the world, including Canada, the United States, Australia, New Zealand, and Europe. He is the recipient of the Marshall McLuhan Distinguished Educator award, an Honorary Fellowship at Scotch College in Melbourne, Australia, and has appeared on City TV's Media Television and TV Ontario's *Parent Connections* as well as in *Computing Now* magazine. Mr. Alger has had the pleasure of working with Apple Computer, Inc., KPMG Canada, The Canadian Film Centre, and The Learning Partnership.

experiencedesigner@yahoo.ca

Acknowledgements

The Experience Designer: Learning, Networks and the Cybersphere is a self-publishing venture. The thoughts and ideas expressed in this book are the sole responsibility of the author. I would like to thank Jerry Durlak, Robin King, and Bob Williams for their encouragement, support, and feedback.
